24

WITHDRAWN

The Language of a Master

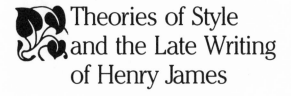

Theories of Style and the Late Writing of Henry James

David W. Smit

Southern Illinois University Press
Carbondale and Edwardsville

Permission to quote from the following sources is gratefully acknowledged.
"The Canal at Rye," by Marvin Bell. Permission of the author.
Material in chapter 4 appeared as "The Later Styles of Henry James," *Style*
  21 (1987):95–106. Permission from the publisher.
Figure 4 is taken from M. A. Just and P. A. Carpenter, "A Theory of Reading:
  From Eye Fixations to Comprehension," *Psychological Review* 87
  (1980):329–54. Permission from M. A. Just.

Library of Congress Cataloging-in-Publication Data

Smit, David William.
  The language of a master.

  Bibliography: p.
  Includes index.
  1. James, Henry, 1843–1916—Style. 2. Style,
Literary. I. Title.
PS2128.S65 1988   813'.4   87-26524
ISBN 0-8093-1399-5

Contents

Illustrations

Tables

Figures

Foreword

The past ten or fifteen years have not been easy ones for those interested in stylistics. From its inception, the discipline, if that is not too grand a term for it, has had its critics, of course, many of whom played variations on René Wellek's observations at the close of the 1958 Indiana Conference on Style that "literary style is to my mind not exhausted by linguistic analysis: it needs analysis in terms of the aesthetic effects toward which it is aiming" and "the danger of linguistic stylistics is its focus on deviations from, and distortions of, the linguistic norm. We get a kind of countergrammar, a science of discards" (p. 417). But these early criticisms suggested their own solutions: one could concentrate less on deviations and more on the recurrent and normal, and one could complement linguistic description with aesthetic analysis. When Jonathan Culler demonstrated, in a detailed consideration of Roman Jakobson's poetic analyses, that linguistic analysis of a text would not uncover its significant patterns and thus could not provide a discovery procedure for stylistics (pp. 55–74), it was still possible to hope that a redirection of the field would solve the problem. Thus Roger Fowler, in "Linguistics, Stylistics; Criticism?" proposed that "the description itself must be purposeful" (p. 154) and M. A. K. Halliday demonstrated how such a purposeful description could be achieved by using a functional grammar in "Linguistic Function and Literary Style: An Inquiry into the Language of William Golding's 'The Inheritors'." Even when Stanley Fish argued, using Halliday as a prime example, that "the absence of any constraint on the way in which one moves from description to interpretation" leads to "the result that any interpretation one puts forward is arbitrary" (pp. 72–73), it was possible to counter the objection by incorporating the reader as an entity whose reactions were guided by (nonarbitrary) linguistic and literary competences, a tack reflected in Jonathan Culler's notion of literary competence and in Roger Fowler's collection of articles entitled *Style and Structure in Literature*, which had the hopeful and perhaps belligerent subtitle *Essays in the New Stylistics.*

But when the essays in this volume were attacked by Barbara Herrnstein Smith in a lengthy review entitled "Surfacing from the Deep," things began to fall apart. Her basic criticism was the same as Fish's: that stylisticians generally posit a relation between some aspect of the text, which may be quite precisely described in terms of linguistic categories, and something more obscure in the work (its theme, artistic design, or whatever) but that the relation between the two, despite the incorporation of the reader, remains problematic and artitrary; the stylisticians, she concluded, seemed "to be running in place at a dead end" (p. 193). Five years after his initial attack, Stanley Fish wrote a companion piece, "What Is Stylistics and Why Are They Saying Such Terrible Things About It? Part II," in which he argued that linguistic analysis was itself a form of interpretation, privileging certain aspects of the language of the text while ignoring others, and so even the formal patterns a linguistic analysis might uncover in a text "are themselves the product of interpretation and . . . therefore there is no such thing as a formal pattern, at least not in the sense necessary for stylistics; that is, no pattern that one can observe before interpretation is hazarded and which therefore can be used to prefer one interpretation to another" (p. 267). And more recently, apparently reflecting the growing feeling that stylistics in anything like its original form was an indefensible enterprise, one of the leading journals in the field, *Style,* has shifted away from its old format of including articles on a number of matters all related in one way or another to the language of texts into a new one in which each issue is devoted to a particular topic, such as "Deconstruction," "Rhythm, Rhetoric, Revision," "Narrative Poetics," "Medieval Semiotics," "Psychopoetics," and "Recent Literary Theory." This growing awareness of the various filiations of stylistics may be applauded, but the reduced emphasis on linguistics and even language indicated how little is left of the exuberant enthusiasm of Whitehall's famous dictum that "as no science can go beyond mathematics, so no criticism can go beyond its linguistics" (p. 415).

Those interested in stylistics have thus been left wondering, in all but words, what, if anything, to make of a diminished thing. David Smit provides one answer in this book. As his subtitle indicates, he has two aims: to reconsider stylistic criticism, and to add some of his own observations to the literature on Henry James. His own stylistic approach is rooted in the kind of "thick description" made popular by the anthropologist Clifford Geertz. The emphasis is on recovering as much of the situation of interpretation as possible: "In order for us to understand how a particular meaning is realized in a particular situation we need to know both the person who understands the language and the situation in which he did so, as well as the codes, rules, or conventions he was bringing into play during that situation." The result is an amalgamation of the older attempts to include the reader within stylistic analyses and the newer emphasis on individual reading experiences typical of reader-response criticism. The "reader" in stylistics—whether the fictionalized Stanley Fish of affective stylistics, the Average Reader or Superreader of Michael Riffaterre's work, or the literarily competent reader in Culler—was primarily a fictional construct, answerable to the rules or conventions or codes that constituted him. In reader-response criticism—especially in Bleich and Holland—the emphasis is less on shared conventions and more on the idiosyncrasy of the individual in a particular psychological and physical context. Smit's position skillfully combines both of these, the "codes, rules, or conventions" echoing the linguistic background, while the "person who understands the language and the situation in which he did so" gestures toward Bleich and Holland: "interpretations of style are the result of an interplay between various codes, rules, or conventions ("shared meanings") and a reader-critic's individual application of these codes, rules, or conventions in a specific context. One of the jobs of stylistics is to make such conventions explicit and to explore how they are applied by different reader-critics in different rhetorical situations." The result is an attractively self-conscious approach to literary language that preserves the notion of a text existing independently of a reader and yet expects different readers to notice different aspects of it.

Style, for Smit, consists of the features a reader notices: "any aspect of the language of a text, any aspect of its diction or syntax, which is used as evidence for a critical assertion or argument about the nature and effect of that language." At first glance, this stipulation seems to have the unfortunate characteristic of not conforming to any earlier definitions of style, which tended to emphasize deviations from some norm, a characteristic way of doing something, or the recurrence of textual units; and it allows the style of a text to vary with the reader. But further consideration reveals the subtlety of Smit's definition, for as his examples indicate, past critics—whatever their theoretical allegiances—have indeed differed in their assessments of the style of a text, which they have indeed identified with a small number of selected textual properties. We may have assumed that this was the result of a constraint on performance—that with more time, and a more forgiving reader, it would be possible to provide as complete a description of the style as desired. But Smit points out that in any situation "we build up . . . a hypothetical concept of the style that is entirely determined by our attention, our experience, and the meaning we derive from the text." Any reading must ignore a large part of what is in the text, even if some kind of checklist of notable linguistic categories is employed to guide the process, simply because the possible categories and their combinations are all but endless, and our attention is not. Smit's definition of style is thus the one critics have been using all along, perhaps unknowingly; what prevents it from being solipsistic is that our experience will often include the work of other critics, and the "meaning we derive from the text" will depend on the conventions, largely shared, that we use to comprehend it.

This view of style is frankly skeptical, skeptical of its own conclusions as well as of what others have said. One of the pleasures of reading this book is the heightened sense of awareness it imparts of the arbitrary nature not only of what other critics have said, but also of our own insights: "our simplest perceptions are conditioned in ways we are barely aware of. The more we make such conventions explicit, the more we realize how little we know ouselves and what "causes" us to read in a particular way." The epigraph to the second chapter is a poem by Marvin Bell that contains lines Smit returns to frequently: "The natural end and extension / of language / is nonsense." Watching David Smit negotiate the extensions and ends of the language of Henry James and of his critics while avoiding the natural end and extension of his own is a bracing and educating experience.

Works Cited

Culler, Jonathan. *Structuralist Poetics.* Ithaca: Cornell Univ. Press, 1975.
Fish, Stanley E. "What Is Stylistics and Why Are They Saying Such Terrible Things About It?" *Is There a Text in This Class?* Cambridge, MA: Harvard Univ. Press, 1980, pp. 68–96.
———. "What Is Stylistics and Why Are They Saying Such Terrible Things About It? Part II." *Is There a Text in this Class?* Cambridge, MA: Harvard Univ. Press, 1980, 246–67.
Fowler, Roger. "Linguistics, Stylistics; Criticism?" *Lingua* 16 (1966):155–65.
Geertz, Clifford. "Thick Description: Toward an Interpretive Theory of Culture," *The Interpretation of Cultures.* New York: Basic Books, 1973, pp. 3–30.
Halliday, M. A. K. "Linguistic Function and Literary Style: An Inquiry into the Language of William Golding's 'The Inheritors'," *Literary Style: A Sym-*

posium, ed. Seymour Chatman. New York: Oxford Univ. Press, 1971, pp. 330–65.

Smith, Barbara Herrnstein. "Surfacing from the Deep," *On The Margins of Discourse.* Chicago: Univ. of Chicago Press, 1978, pp. 157–201.

Wellek, René. "Closing Statement: From the Viewpoint of Literary Criticism," *Style in Language,* ed. Thomas A. Sebeok. Cambridge, MA: M.I.T. Press, 1960, pp. 408–19.

Whitehall, Harold. "From Linguistics to Criticism." *Kenyon Review* 18 (1956):411–21.

Acknowledgements

 I would like to thank the following people for the time and energy they devoted to reading and commenting on this book: Judith Aikin, Paul Diehl, Eugene Kintgen, David Morrell, and Carole de Saint Victor.

My thanks also to the editors and staff of the Southern Illinois University Press, who were unfailingly courteous, patient, and helpful in the preparation of the manuscript. I would especially like to thank Robert Phillips, the Editorial Director, and Joyce Atwood, the Senior Editor.

Above all, I would like to thank Brooks Landon, whose early comments on the manuscript made me realize what it means to belong to a community of scholars and whose enthusiasm and faith in the manuscript kept me going.

Abbreviations

References to the works of Henry James are to the following standard editions unless otherwise noted.

AMB   *The Ambassadors.* "The New York Edition." New York: Charles Scribner's Sons, 1909.

ART   *The Art of the Novel.* Ed. R. P. Blackmur. New York: Charles Scribner's Sons, 1962.

BIJ   "The Beast in the Jungle," in *The Complete Tales of Henry James.* Vol. 11. London: Rupert Hart- Davis, 1964.

FN   *The Future of the Novel.* Ed. Leon Edel. New York: Vintage Books, 1956.

GB   *The Golden Bowl.* "The New York Edition." New York: Charles Scribner's Sons, 1909.

ITC   "In the Cage," in *What Maisie Knew and Other Tales.* "The New York Edition." New York: Charles Scribner's Sons, 1909.

LET   *The Letters of Henry James.* Vol. 1. Ed. Percy Lubbock. New York: Octagon Books, 1970.

NOT   *The Notebooks of Henry James.* Ed. F. O. Matthiessen and Kenneth B. Murdock. New York: Oxford Univ. Press, 1961.

SA   "The Saint's Afternoon," in *Italian Hours.* New York: Grove Press, Inc., n.d.

SF   *The Sacred Fount.* New York: Grove Press, 1953.

SY   "The Story of a Year," in *The Complete Tales of Henry James.* Vol. 1. Ed. Leon Edel. London: Rupert Hart-Davis, 1962.

TE   "A Tragedy of Error," in *The Complete Tales of Henry James.*
          Vol. 1. Ed. Leon Edel. London: Rupert Hart-Davis, 1962.

TF   "The Two Faces," in *The Complete Tales of Henry James.*
          Vol. 11. Ed. Leon Edel. London: Rupert Hart-Davis, 1969.

WOD   *The Wings of the Dove.* "The New York Edition." New York:
          Charles Scribner's Sons, 1909.

The Language of a Master

1. *Introduction*

"There's an idea in my work without which I wouldn't have given a straw for the whole job. It's the finest, fullest intention of the lot, and the application of it has been, I think, a triumph of patience, of ingenuity. I ought to leave that to somebody else to say; but that nobody does say it is precisely what we're talking about. It stretches, this little trick of mine, from book to book, and everything else, comparatively, plays over the surface of it. The order, the form, the texture of my books will perhaps some day constitute for the initiated a complete representation of it. So it's naturally the thing for the critic to look for. It strikes me," my visitor added, smiling, "even as the thing for the critic to find."

I scratched my head. "Is it something in the style or something in the thought? An element of form or an element of feeling?"

He indulgently shook my hand again, and I felt my questions to be crude and my distinctions pitiful. "Good-night, my dear boy—don't bother about it. After all, you do like a fellow."

"And a little intelligence might spoil it?" I still detained him.

He hesitated. "Well, you've got a heart in your body. Is that an element of form or an element of feeling? What I contend that nobody has ever mentioned in my work is the organ of life."

"I see—it's some idea about life, some sort of philosophy. Unless it be," I added with the eagerness of a thought perhaps still happier, "some kind of game you're up to with your style, something you're after in the language. Perhaps it's a preference for the letter P!" I ventured profanely to break out. "Papa, potatoes, prunes— that sort of thing?" He was suitably indulgent: he only said I hadn't got the right letter. But his amusement was over: I could see that he was bored.

—"The Figure in the Carpet"

Reading these words from "The Figure in the Carpet," I can not help but envision Henry James at his writing desk, presciently imagining how critics in the future would try to come to grips with his late style and deciding, early, to put them in their place. Of course, my vision is pure fancy. For one thing, in 1896, the year he wrote "The Figure in the Carpet," James had not yet begun to write in his celebrated late style. For another, because of the lightly exaggerated tone of James' story, it is not clear who or what is being satirized, if anyone or anything is being satirized at all. Certainly by modern critical standards the nameless narrator seems rather ridiculous for believing in a distinction between form and feeling, for believing that the style of a great author can be reduced to a preference for *p*'s. James seems to be having a great deal of fun at his narrator's expense. But I think it is important to note that the narrator gets his idea of a single critical principle which can illuminate an entire body of work from Hugh Verecker, the great writer himself—and thus James may be ridiculing Verecker just as much as he is ridiculing the narrator. Verecker's claim of a single "little trick" that informs "the order, the form, the texture" of his books sounds like a trap for the naïve, the critical equivalent of the philosopher's stone or "the secret of the universe." James carries his satire through to the end of the story, at which time Verecker is dead, the critic who claimed to have discovered the single "little trick" is also dead, and the narrator in his fanatical quest for the secret is forced to interrogate the second husband of the critic's wife for any clues to the secret—only to learn that she did not share it, that all the ways of determining the secret by external biographical means are closed: we must take the author's word that a single critical principle informs his work, and all we can do to determine the principle is to read his work, consider various hypotheses, and live with uncertainty. Verecker's "little trick" may indeed be a great truth—but it may also be a great absurdity, an author's harsh joke on an overly eager, overly impressionable audience with its questions crude and its distinctions pitiful.

I begin a study of James' style with "The Figure in the Carpet" because nowadays we tend to take James and his way of writing very seriously indeed, much the same way that the narrator of "The Figure" takes Hugh Verecker. We consider James a master and more often than not treat him as a saint or even an icon, something hard and fixed to be worshiped rather than appreciated, his style the manifestation of a great critical principle, "a triumph of patience, of ingenuity." In this atmosphere I think it wise to remind ourselves that James had a sense of ambiguity and a sense of humor, that he himself could recognize his propensity for certain forms such as alliteration, which may or may not indicate an underlying vision, that his use of language was human, not perfect, and therefore subject to the same constraints as the language we all use.

Style, of course, is one of those terms that continues to confound us, and perhaps of all styles Jamesian style confounds us most completely. Definitions of style abound, and theoretical justifications for various uses of the term are almost as common as definitions. No two definitions refer to quite the same aspect of language, and no two theories of style provide exactly the same view of how style functions in discourse as a whole. And yet, somehow, we all know what we mean by style, even if we cannot pin the term down, and when we talk about James' late style we all know what we are referring to. We are referring to expository writing like this:

> Really, universally, relations stop nowhere, and the exquisite problem of the artist is eternally but to draw, by a geometry of his own, the circle within which they shall happily *appear* to do so. He is in the perpetual predicament that the continuity of things is the whole matter, for him, of comedy and tragedy; that this continuity is never, by the space of an instant or an inch, broken, and that, to do anything at all, he has at once intensely to consult and intensely to ignore it. All of which will perhaps pass but for a supersubtle way of pointing the plain moral that a young embroiderer of the canvas of life soon began to work in terror, fairly, of the vast expanse of that surface, of the boundless number of its distinct perforations for the needle, and of the tendency inherent in his many-coloured flowers and figures to cover and consume as many as possible of the little holes. (*ART,* 5)

And we are referring to fictional writing like this:

> It all left her, as she wandered off, with the strangest of impressions—the sense, forced upon her as never yet, of an appeal, a positive confidence, from the four pairs of eyes, that was deeper than any negation, and that seemed to speak, on the part of each, of some relation to be contrived by her, a relation with herself, which would spare the individual the danger, the actual present strain, of the relation with the others. They thus

tacitly put it upon her to be disposed of, the whole complexity of
their peril, and she promptly saw why: because she was there,
and there just *as* she was, to lift it off them and take it; to charge
herself with it as the scapegoat of old, of whom she had once
seen a terrible picture, had been charged with the sins of the
people and had gone forth into the desert to sink under his
burden and die. (*GB*, II, 234)

After an hour or two of reading such prose, we may be tempted to
throw up our hands in exasperation and exclaim, much as William
James did in a letter to Henry: "The method seems perverse: 'Say it
out, for God's sake.' They [your worthy readers] cry, 'and have done
with it.'"[1] James' late style with its unusual diction and sentence structure is a concrete example of the most fundamental issue raised by
the various definitions and theories of style: whether style is the same
thing as "meaning." The issue is debated endlessly by theorists of
language and literature: can style be changed without changing the
"meaning"? That is, should we infer that what James wrote is exactly
what he meant, that his method is his message? Or should we, as
implied by brother William, hypothetically separate James' method
from his "meaning" and determine from our own reading whether James
could have said the same thing better, more forcefully, more clearly,
with different words? The answers to these questions are many and
complex, and I bring them up once again because it seems to me that
the critical response to James' late style has been—to put it bluntly—
rather glib. The fact that James wrote like no one else has been taken
as a sign of his genius. The probability that we would deplore anyone
else writing like him is conveniently overlooked. Evaluations and justifications of James' style are often fanciful, even silly, and just as often
theoretically naïve, transparent attempts to provide any sort of explanation for a style that is dense, hard to read, and notoriously difficult
to explain. In short, I have yet to read a convincing aesthetic or thematic
rationale for James' late style, and I cannot provide one now, although
I can give a psychological explanation for why James wrote as he did.
Therefore, I propose to examine a variety of critical responses to James'
late style in the light of stylistic theory in order to point out what I
consider their inadequacies and to indicate what shape an adequate
explanation of an author's style should take. Basically, I will advance
the following argument:

    The notion of style would be a more useful concept in criticism if
we conceived of it, not as a set of formal features in a text, but as the

result of a reader-critic's perception of the text, as those features in a text that provide the evidence for the critic's attitude or argument. Each of us recognizes different aspects of James' style for different reasons, depending on our background and critical interest, depending on the attitude we have toward James or the critical hypothesis we are pursuing. Those aspects of James' style we set forth, then, will be entirely determined by the rhetorical situation in which we recognized them, in which we decided their significance, and in which we decided to present them as relevant to a particular point of view or argument. Our recognition of certain stylistic features may take place instantaneously or over time, but in any case we notice certain aspects of style and not others for reasons of our own, and I think we would further the process of critical discussion if we frankly acknowledged that in any given situation we are talking not about James' style as it really is but about our perception of James' style, with the attendant obligation to explain our critical methods and the rules or conventions that determine the meaning of the terms we use. Indeed, it seems to me that all interpretations of a style are the result of an interplay between various codes, rules, or conventions ("shared meanings") and a reader-critic's individual application of these codes, rules, or conventions in a specific context. One of the jobs of stylistics is to make such conventions explicit and to explore how they are applied by different reader-critics in different rhetorical situations. Roland Barthes' metaphor is revealing: a work of art is like an onion, "a construction of layers (or levels, or systems)," not a fruit with a pit at the center. After we have stripped away the layers of what Barthes calls codes, there is no "work of art itself" left. To Barthes, a prose style is the sum of the codes, rules, or conventions with which we perceive and analyze it.[2] To which I would add only one qualification: a prose style is the sum of how various codes, rules, or conventions are realized by each reader-critic who applies them; a prose style is the result of a constant and complex tension between particular contexts and more general conventions.

My own definition of style, therefore, tries to encompass all the various ways in which I see the term being used in the critical response to James. For this study, I define style as any aspect of the language of a text, any aspect of its diction or syntax, which is used as evidence for a critical assertion or argument about the nature and effect of that language. I see critics of James asserting three major claims for his late style: that it is unique, that it is expressive, that it is thematically relevant. Perhaps a few examples might help to clarify what I mean by these terms. If we assert that James' prose is characterized by intangible nouns and odd parenthetical interruptions in the syntax, we are arguing that those characteristics make James' prose distinctive or unique or at least recognizably written by James. I call such assertions Style as Identification, and I discuss the difficulties with such claims about James' late style in chapter 3. In this chapter I show that James' fiction is sufficiently various at the level at which most stylistic analysis takes place so that we would be hard pressed to recognize much of James' late style as distinctively Jamesian. If we assert that James' prose is "eloquent" or "obscure" or that it illustrates the fundamental way in which he perceived reality, we are arguing that various aspects of a text "express" an aesthetic quality or an aspect of an author's personality. I call these assertions Style as Expression, and I deal with these claims about James' late style in chapter 4. In this chapter I point out the difficulties of associating various features of the late style with such aesthetic qualities as "eloquence," and I analyze five kinds of writing that James did in the winter of 1899–1900. The results of my analysis indicate that James' writing is so various we cannot associate any particular aspect of his style with his personality, that various rhetorical critics are right: all writing is the assumption of a mask, a *persona*, an implied author. I also explore the implications of this analysis by speculating why, psychologically, James might have wanted to adopt the "voice" of the late style as a mask. Finally, if we assert that James' language, say his parenthetical interruptions, are especially appropriate to his rendering of the mental life of his characters, that complex sentences interrupted by parentheses are an intrinsically better way to convey the workings of the mind than simple declarative sentences, then we are asserting that language can "imitate" or be appropriate to the subject matter. I call these assertions Style as Imitation, and I deal with such claims as applied to James in chapter 5. In this chapter I trace the way James portrayed mental process in his fiction from his earliest stories up to the late style, and I show that those features which critics usually associate with the mental life of the characters are present in James' early stories, that they are qualities not of the characters but of James' narrative voice.

Certainly there are other reasons for noticing various aspects of the language of literary texts: linguists may note the way a text coheres or the way the dialogue indicates the socioeconomic class of the characters, structuralists may note the underlying pattern of the plot and how it exemplifies a fundamental way of organizing human experience, more traditional critics may notice certain motifs and allusions to history or mythology. All of these approaches refer to style in Richard

Ohmann's sense of "a way of doing it."[3] In each case I think we ought to grant the critic his definition of style in order to see what use he can make of it. For this study of James, however, I would like to focus on Style as Identification, Style as Expression, and Style as Imitation because it seems to me that in critical explanations of James' style these three ways of talking about style pay the most attention to the language of the text and try to arrive at the most comprehensive explanations for what James' writing is like and what it does. Also, in many cases the underlying assumptions and critical procedures of these three kinds of explanations are not explicit.

I propose, then, to analyze each of these ways of explaining James' late style in order to point out its rationale, its set of assumptions, and its rules of evidence. If I can clarify what these assumptions and rules of evidence are, we ought to be able to judge more clearly how well each of these critical methods explains James' style.

Even if we grant the validity of each of these methods of explaining James' style, I think we will find it difficult to account for the late style, except psychologically. The situations in which James used the late style indicate that he most often adopted the "voice" or "tone" of that style when he wanted to be an artist, when he wanted to speak in an "aesthetic mode," when he wanted to play the role of "the master." There are many reasons why James would have wanted to assume such a role, consciously or not, the most obvious being that he was a very shy man in many ways and a magisterial tone was one way of asserting himself. In any case, I plan to show the difficulties of justifying the late style aesthetically or thematically, so that a psychological explanation becomes the only one we have without such difficulties.

This lack of an aesthetic or thematic rationale for the late style has clear implications for stylistic theory. The assumption that prose can be analyzed with the same minute scrutiny as poetry and achieve thereby the same rewarding results becomes questionable: a word-for-word justification of any prose style may not be possible. I explore the implications of this judgment in the conclusion by examining the assumptions and methods of a great piece of stylistic criticism, Ian Watt's "First Paragraph of *The Ambassadors*: An Explication." Despite the detail and elegance of Watt's argument, whether we appreciate James' late style or not may be less a matter of critical insight and rigor than a matter of taste.

2. *Theories of Style*

Turn back
to art, including the sentence.
It is also the world.   Whoever understands
the sentence understands
his or her life.   There are reasons
not to, reasons too
to believe or not to.   But
reasons do not complete an argument.
The natural end and extension
of language
is nonsense.   Yet there is safety
only there.   That is why Mr. Henry James
wrote that way—
out with the tide, but further.

Marvin Bell, "The Canal at Rye"

"The natural end and extension / of language / is nonsense. Yet there is safety / only there." I take it that Marvin Bell is talking not just about James' language, literary language, but about all language, including the language of criticism. Language is an arbitrary code with no necessary or logical connection to reality as we experience it through our senses. True, language is governed by a series of rules or grammars, but these rules are in themselves conventions with no necessary or logical connection to reality. To think about language at all is to confront an infinite hall of mirrors in which diction and syntax, rules of grammar, the neurological structure of the human mind, and what we call reality reflect upon one another with no ultimate source for all the shifting mirror images. We understand language as we can, as we must, as we want to: "There are reasons / not to, reasons too / to believe or not to." One of the reasons we read Henry James, as well as other great writers, is to watch a master of language come to terms with the limits imposed on him by the nature of things, to watch him test those limits, creating in the process a new prism for viewing the hall or, an even greater achievement, creating a new addition to the hall, a new reality, risking all the while complete and total nonsense. So too, I think, we read and write criticism: to come to terms with great writers, to test our perception and knowledge against what they have created for us, to explore the limits of our own understanding. In Bell's metaphor, both writers and critics try to discover the natural end and extension of language where the sentence and the world become nonsense but where, paradoxically, we must all seek our safety, a place beyond the confines of the shore.

If we want to talk about style at all, and James' style in particular, we need some ground to stand on, some position from which to view the mirror images. A great deal of critical ground, it seems to me, has been off in a small corner, providing a very limited view.

Critical evaluations of James' late style are of two kinds, reflecting a major difference of opinion and method in the field of stylistics as a whole. On the one hand are the traditional personal responses to James' language by literary critics, who relate the style to larger thematic and philosophical concerns, often to their notion of James' "vision." The other camp calls this approach "impressionism." Be that as it may, the major works of Jamesian criticism are of this kind. Thus, Laurence Holland can speak of James' writing as an example of "mannerism" which is appropriate to James' view of reality:

> [James'] manner characterizes not only the surface textures of the prose in its energetic twisting and distended tautness—but also the extended reach of his themes and characterization and the foundation of the fiction's movement and architecture. The author, like the dramatist, is screened from view in the wings, but the movement of the drama, its objective presence and style, become conspicuous, stand in bold relief. The style becomes an instrument for the rendering of characters and themes which range in import beyond what was customary in the novel of manners. . . . His form is distinct and tangible yet more plastic than generically denotative or emblematic prose, aiming beyond the given specifications of actuality, emblems, and types toward a new reality which is the offspring of what it finds and what it makes.[1]

Holland is as explicit as any major critic of James in justifying the late style. He characterizes the style—"its energetic twisting and distended tautness"; it is "distinct and tangible yet more plastic than generically denotative or emblematic prose"—and he asserts that such a style is necessary for "the extended reach of his [James'] themes and characterization and the foundation of the fiction's movement and architecture." Except for a few isolated examples in other contexts, however, he offers no evidence for his assertions. Other critics are content merely to characterize James' prose. F. O. Matthiessen in his essay on James' revisions of *The Portrait of a Lady* refers to "the solemnities of his mandarin style." Matthiessen's careful explanation of the revisions—that they "sharpen the reader's impression of how incorrigibly romantic Isabel's approach to life is," that they are more colloquial, more concrete, and contain more analogies with pictures and painting than the original, that they show more delight in virtuosity—does not really account for his judgment that James' style is solemn and mandarin, however.[2] Joseph Warren Beach, another eminent critic of James, does not describe the features of James' style at all; yet he characterizes the style this way:

> [James] is never sarcastic, never lachrymose, never moralistic. There is never any suffusion of his work with a cosmic poesy such as distinguishes the work of Hardy. It is always unmistakably the tone of prose in which he speaks. He has but a mild tincture of that gusto—that blend of irony and boyish high spirits—that makes the family likeness of male English novelists from Fielding to Scott to Dickens and Meredith. The tone of James is the tone of indoors and the tea-table. There is about him no smell of peat or sagebrush. You cannot imagine him peddling Bibles in Spain or 'squatting' in California among the rattlesnakes. You cannot imagine him taking an interest in the soul of a planter up some river in Borneo. His words are never scattered and disarranged by any breath of the boisterous Atlantic.[3]

Austin Warren gives James high praise by imitating him, but he too merely characterizes the prose: "Henry's later manner is an allegro slowed down to a largo, the conversational in apotheosis. 'Literary' as, all sprinkled with its commas of parenthesis, it looks on paper, it is an oral style; and, verifiably, it becomes clear, almost luminous, if recommitted to the voice."[4]

Such impressions of James' late style need not be positive. F. R. Leavis finds the style lacking in "full-bodied life," a judgment Leavis supports with a single example from *The Golden Bowl*.

Just three things in themselves, however, with all the rest, with his fixed purpose now, his committed deed, the fine pink glow, projected forward, of his ships, behind him, definitely blazing and crackling—this quantity was to push him harder than any word of his own could warn him. All that she was herself, moreover, was so lighted, to its advantage, by the pink glow.

Leavis comments that "this hasn't the concrete immediacy of metaphor; it is, rather, coloured diagram."[5]

Opposed to such eloquent impressions of James' work are more precise linguistic descriptions, which claim to document or validate the subjectivity of the literary critics or to offer a more "objective" kind of interpretation, a kind of interpretation which rises organically and even necessarily out of the "objective data" of the text. The impressionists find this approach heavy in terminology and trivial in result. Indeed, many linguistic analyses of James' late prose are quite short: the critics doing these analyses seem less interested in explicating James than they do in using his work as an example of how a particular system of linguistic analysis functions. Thus in one essay Richard Ohmann applies a generative-transformational model of language to one sentence from "The Bench of Desolation" in order to show how deletions of deep-structure sentences and the self-embedding of grammatical elements can account for one aspect of James' style.[6] Roger Fowler uses an analysis of a paragraph from *The Ambassadors* to illustrate his thesis that style can reflect the qualities of consciousness; in this case, that James' nominalization of adjectives and predicates suggests "inactivity, repression of the agency function, reduction in the strength of the will in those human characters to whom this style is applied."[7] And Geoffrey Leech and Michael Short in their text *Style in Fiction* use a passage from "The Pupil" to illustrate the application of various linguistic categories—their main discovery after fourteen pages of laying out various features of the text, everything from clause structure to irony and context, is that the passage contains shifts in register "to give a multidimensional sense of situation." Following Fowler, Leech and Short also use a passage from "The Birthplace" as an example of "mind style": in the passage they cite, a long noun phrase and various abstract nouns and adjectives suggest the character's personality, attitude, and social standing rather than his physical appearance.[8]

A large number of articles and doctoral dissertations continue the method: a minute categorizing of textual features, often with elaborate statistics showing how often the features occur, accompanied by little critical judgment about what all the data mean.[9]

The best and most complete linguistic description of James' late style is by Seymour Chatman in his book *The Later Style of Henry James*. Chatman is nothing if not thorough. He carefully delineates eighteen aspects of James' prose, everything from its abstract diction to obliquity, deixis, ellipsis, and expletives *it* and *there*. To be certain the features are typically Jamesian he compares the occurrence of key features with four other novels of the period. Thus we learn that in sample passages of 196 to 200 sentences James uses intangible grammatical subjects virtually half the time, while Gissing, Forster, Butler, and Conrad have humans as the grammatical subject 67 percent of the time.[10] But like many other linguistic critics Chatman is less clear about what all his information means. His stated purpose is to clearly establish a basis for judging which of various parodies of James is the most accurate, and that he does very thoroughly. But in the process of establishing a general model for James' style, Chatman offers a number of judgments of that style, almost as if he felt an obligation to make something more of his wealth of data.[11]

The different methods of the impressionist and linguistic critics of James reflect a larger split in the practice of stylistics as a discipline. As early as 1937 René Wellek in an otherwise favorable review of *Revaluation* called on F. R. Leavis to state his assumptions "more explicitly" and defend them "systematically," a task which Leavis rejected as inappropriate to the practice of criticism:

> Words in poetry invite us not to "think about" and judge, but to "feel into" or "become"—to realize a complex experience that is given in the words. . . . The critic—the reader of poetry—is indeed concerned with evaluation, but to figure him as measuring with a norm which he brings up to the object and applies from outside is to misrepresent the process. The critic's aim is, first, to realize as sensitively and completely as possible this or that which claims his attention: and a certain valuing is implicit in the realizing.[12]

Despite the fact that Wellek was not then and is not now primarily a linguistic critic—at the Indiana Conference on Style in 1958 he quite sharply distinguished where linguistic analysis ends and criticism begins—he and Leavis illustrate the two opposing views of stylistic criticism. Leavis believes that critical judgment is the result of intuition and of making explicit how the literary work claims the critic's attention. Wellek believes that criticism ought to be much more rational and principled, systematic in its application of method, and thus, Wellek finds a great deal of linguistic analysis useful.[13]

The disagreement is carried on today by the practitioners of the New Stylistics, led by Roger Fowler, and other critics such as Stanley Fish and Barbara Herrnstein Smith. Fowler proclaims linguistic techniques to be "a precise instrument of textual description" and "very much like traditional literary criticism (but methodologically and theoretically superior!) in interpreting texts for whose language and ideas it has great respect."[14] Fish and Smith respond by granting that linguistic descriptions of texts are precise, but they deny that the method is any different from traditional criticism in producing critical judgments, with the exception that a fascination with linguistic detail often leads linguistic critics to overvalue certain aspects of the text which results in turn in ludicrously overblown claims for their interpretations.[15] It is noteworthy that when he is confronted with the charge that linguistic criticism may have advanced the cause of description but not of evaluation, Fowler argues that there is at present no completely adequate theory of style, and he—like all of the practitioners of the discipline since it began—offers a number of areas for further exploration, holding out the possibility that an adequate theory of style is just around the corner.[16] I think that Fowler's defense avoids the key issues. It seems to me that we have any number of theories of style, each of which is useful for its own particular purposes, and I plan to summarize them in a moment. We also have any number of aesthetic theories which argue that what Fowler wants, a clearly stated, logically necessary way to move from description to evaluation, is impossible, and I will present these arguments in subsequent chapters. Fowler, of course, does not confront the issue of whether his vision of "an adequate theory of style" is even possible.

Because theorists of style often promote their own theories at the expense of others and because *style* is such a slippery term to begin with, it is not surprising that the impressionists and the linguists disagree so passionately. But it seems to me that their differences are relatively minor, that both camps have an inadequate notion of style, and that their inadequacies stem from a common fault: both sides conceive of style as a collection of formal properties in the text; neither side has an epistemology that recognizes the role of the critic in perceiving, ordering, and interpreting these properties in a meaningful manner. Linguists focus so heavily on the data of their descriptions that they fail to see how subjective and loaded with assumptions and biases their supposedly objective analyses really are, as when William Smith counts the number of complex sentences in James' stories in order to prove that the style becomes increasingly complex.[17] Smith assumes that complex ideas must of necessity be expressed in complex sentences, a questionable assumption that Smith does not bother to argue. Literary critics, on the other hand, are so involved in their personal interpretations that they justify the data in odd ways and use the language of empiricism to disguise personal aesthetic judgments. Barry Menikoff, for example, asserts that James' use of the dash and colon simulate "the process of the mind, the manner in which we apprehend ideas," but Menikoff feels no obligation to offer evidence that our minds do in fact work as a model for James' use of punctuation.[18] In short, most of the analyses of James' style would be much clearer and more convincing if they made explicit the ways in which reader-critics manipulate the formal properties of a text for their own purposes. What we need to ask in the case of each critical analysis is not "What are the formal properties of the text?" but "Who is doing the analysis? Under what circumstances? What method is being used? And above all, What are these formal properties being used for?"

Traditional theories of style, then, are inadequate because they neglect the rhetorical situation in favor of a universal concept of style, even though such a concept does not exist, and a universal theory of "meaning," even though "meaning," except for broad strategies for interpretation, is entirely determined by particular people in particular situations. Consider these ideas of style. There is the notion of style as those elements which a text shares with others by the same author or with others in the same genre or the same period; thus we speak of Jamesian style, dramatic style, and Romantic style. There is the notion of style as an indication of social class or register; thus we speak of black style or formal style. There is the notion of style as a proper or correct means of expression; thus we speak of good or bad style. There is the popular notion of style as synonymous with "kind"; thus we speak of revising a passage in a different style, much as we would speak of a chair coming in two styles—in leather or Herculon. Finally, there is the notion of style as simply those features in a text which we want to pay attention to; thus we speak of a style being full of allusion or metaphor. All of these notions of style are related to each other by what Wittgenstein called family-resemblance.[19] There is no central or core meaning. The difficulty we all have in using the term "style" is not that we do not use the word with precision but that the term is such an umbrella to take in such a wide range of related concepts that despite our most careful preliminary definitions we often find ourselves using the term in any number of senses quite different from our original definition, and quite correctly, too. Our usage in particular cases is usually quite precise and accurate; it is the way our usage shifts from case to case that is so bothersome. No theory of style will be comprehensive until it encompasses all of these notions of style.

Meaning, of course, is just as contentious a concept as *style*. The problem of meaning is as old as the subject-object distinction or the interplay of rhetoric and dialectic. A great deal of recent critical debate has placed the meaning of a literary work either in the text, the experience of readers, or the interpretive conventions of the community a reader belongs to. The New Critics, of course, with their notions of the intentional and affective fallacies, placed the meaning of the text in the text itself.[20] As far as I know, Louise Rosenblatt was the first modern critic to call this position into question with the notion that meaning was the result of a "transaction" between the text and the reader.[21] The idea that meaning is the result of the interaction of a reader with a text has been taken up by more recent theorists such as Roman Ingarden and Wolfgang Iser, who argue that the reader fills in "gaps" or "indeterminacies" in the text; nevertheless, to both Ingarden and Iser the text "structures" the reader's response.[22] More subjective critics such as Norman Holland and David Bleich assign meaning to the reader: for Holland, the reader discovers an "identity theme" in the text; for Bleich, "meaning" results from the personal associations and values which a reader attaches to the text.[23] Stanley Fish, on the other hand, promotes meaning as a function of the interpretive strategies of a given interpretive community.[24] Despite the recent controversy, the main issues of the debate have been perennial problems in philosophy since the beginning of the discipline. Perhaps the most popular formulation of the issue in contemporary criticism is René Wellek and Austin Warren's *Theory of Literature*. Wellek and Warren consider the literary work a structure of norms, analogous to the phoneme. Just as no two pronunciations of the sound /p/ are exactly the same and yet we all are able to distinguish what the sound is, so also no two readings of a literary work are exactly the same and yet we all know what we are referring to when we talk about our responses to, say, "The Beast in the Jungle." Wellek and Warren do not resolve the paradox of where "meaning" resides in a literary work, but they clearly state the possibilities.[25] To Wellek and Warren there must be a norm for us to refer to in discussing literature, but on the other hand, the norm can only be realized in particular readings by particular readers at particular times. The very use of the term *norm*, however, indicates where Wellek and Warren stand on the issue. To them the work of art must constrain or control the way we read it. It is this assertion which has come under fire by reader-response critics and deconstructionists and which has been the result of intense research in the reading process and cognitive psychology. There does not seem to be any reason inherent in the words of a text itself to account for opposing interpretations of the very same words—for example, a straightforward reading or an ironic one opposed to it. The only constraint is the words themselves, the fact that they are not other words. But once we grant this one constraint or control over how we read, the possible interpretations of what a given text can mean and do are infinite, as various as the codes, rules, and conventions—linguistic, literary, cultural, historical, political, and biographical for both author and reader—that we can put into play in any given situation. Thus for all practical purposes any discussion of *meaning* must be in the context of a particular rhetorical situation, in terms of the intention of a particular person in using language in a particular situation, the effect that language has on a particular audience, or if we are thinking metacritically, in terms of the codes, rules, or conventions—the "shared" meanings—which give that language significance in the first place. These codes are not just linguistic but also cognitive and perceptual, as well as literary, cultural, and historical, any convention that allows us to construct our own reality and share it with someone else.

Traditional theories of style fall into three major schools—dualism, psychological monism, and aesthetic monism. Because they all use a very general notion of style and only one definition of meaning, these theories are not contradictory but complementary. Taken alone, each of these theories is inadequate, but together they present a comprehensive notion of how style relates to meaning.

In the view of dualists, the intention of the writer is prior to and "deeper" than his expression of it, and therefore, a single intention can be expressed in a variety of ways, as shown in figure 1. Style in this view is a kind of ornament, and changing the ornament does not change the basic intention of the writer. Dualism has been widely perceived as a necessary theory for specialists in composition, who need to distinguish between intention and style in order to promote the process of revision among their students, so they can say, "Are

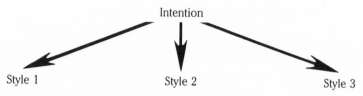

Fig. 1. Style and intention in dualism.

you sure this means what you want to say? Why not try saying it another way?" To proponents of dualism, style is not meaning in the sense that the way we say something must be distinguished from what we really intend.[26] As far as I know, there are no literary critics of James who actively argue the dualistic view, but the assumptions of the dualistic theory are implicit in all criticism of James' late style which suggests that it could be done differently. Brother William's protests that Henry 7could write more clearly if he wanted to imply the dualistic view.

To psychological monists such as Benedetto Croce intentions can only be embodied in particular expressions, and therefore, any change in style implies a change in intention, as shown in figure 2.

Because Croce does not distinguish between intention and effect, he often seems to assert the absurd position that a mental intention prior to expression must be identical to the precise verbal expression of that intention: to allow for a difference would be to admit the dualist position.[27] Thus Croce must argue that the exact wording and punctuation of a text embody the author's intentions before he wrote the words down and, therefore, to change a single word or mark of punctuation is tantamount to changing the writer's fundamental mental concept or vision. Once again, I know of no critic of James who declares himself to be a psychological monist, but the assumptions of psychological monism are implicit in those arguments in favor of James' style on the grounds that it embodies his intentions: for example, in Wayne Booth's argument that we can trust the narrator of "The Turn of the Screw" because "surely James' intentions are clear: he is attempting one of his lucid—but of course not *too* lucid—reflectors."[28]

Fig. 2. Style and intention in psychological monism.

Since we know that intention or "deep structure" meaning is often imagistic, nonverbal, associative, and subject to its own rules, of which we understand very little, psychological monism is not a popular theory. But the notion that style is identical with meaning has been taken over by the aesthetic monists, who make the theory more convincing by defining meaning as effect. Aesthetic monists, represented in America by the New Critics, would argue that an author's intentions are irrelevant in determining the meaning of a literary work, or at least they are only worth talking about as they are embodied in the particular forms of language he chose, and therefore, it is more helpful to talk about "the intentions of the literary work" rather than the intentions of the author. Since the intentions of the author are inaccessible except as embodied in the particular work, we can only talk about the work itself, which means in reality talking about the effect of the work on particular readers (see fig. 3).

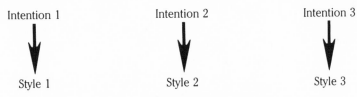

Intention 1   Intention 2   Intention 3

Style 1   Style 2   Style 3

Fig. 3.   Style and effect in aesthetic monism.

If a difference in a stylistic feature—the substitution of a synonym, for example—affects us differently, then by definition, style is meaning and a change in style will result in a change in meaning.[29] Almost all the critics of James' late style are avowed aesthetic monists. Their perception that a change in wording would affect them differently is their primary evidence in favor of James' style. Thus Ian Watt can argue in his brilliant essay on the first paragraph of *The Ambassadors* that "most newly disembarked" means something rather different from "more newly disembarked" and that James was right to use the former.[30]

Because these traditional theories do not define style very carefully, any of the notions of style which I cited earlier could be used in each of the theories. Whether in each case style was meaning would depend on particular usage. If we think of *ain't*, for example, as part of the style of certain social groups in the United States and if we take the stand of the aesthetic monists that a change in style is a change in effect, clearly if a person eliminates *ain't* from his speech or writing, he may cause his audience to think of him as belonging to a different social class. Style, in this case, is meaning. If, on the other hand, we take the dualistic view and define meaning as intention, there may be no difference in the intent of a writer or speaker between "That ain't so" and "That isn't true." Style, in this case, is not meaning—unless the speaker or writer *intends* for us to notice his difference in social status. James' many revisions give us ample opportunity to consider whether his changes embody the same intent or a different one, or whether the newer version affects us differently than the original. What, for example, are we to make of this change of words for the New York edition of *The Portrait of a Lady*? At one point in that novel James changed "She looked brilliant and noble" to "She looked high and splendid."[31] We could argue, in one sense, that these terms are synonymous and, in another sense, that they are quite different.

Much of what we now know about the cognitive processes involved in communication indicates that the views of the dualists and the aesthetic monists are not contradictory but complementary. Ever since William James first focused attention on the problem in *The Principles of Psychology* we have known that mental processes are largely unconscious and nonverbal and that intention is the shaping of these processes in ways largely unknown to us.[32] Therefore, we cannot necessarily equate "intention" with a particular verbal utterance or a written product. We make slips of the tongue or pen; sometimes words are simply intractable, and however aware we are of realizing our intention, we have to settle for the meaning the words allow us. Recent research in the practice of composing has also shown us that a great deal of "intention" is often realized at the moment the words are going onto the paper or the video screen, what James Britton calls "the point of utterance."[33]

On the other hand, everything we have learned about reading in the past twenty years indicates that what we retain from reading is highly selective and dependent upon our own consciousness, which in turn is dependent upon our own experience and previous knowledge organized into what reading theorists call schemata. Research in reading posits the interaction of two processes as we read, bottom-up and top-down, and both are dependent on the attention and previous knowledge of the reader. We take in the words on the page selectively in a rough sequential order, but we store the "meaning" in short-term memory, then later in long-term memory, according to larger schemas of what we already know and our particular purposes at the time.[34] Figure 4, for example, presents a model of the reading process.[35] Notice in this model how the working memory assigns "meaning" to the features of the text according to the previous knowledge of the reader and how

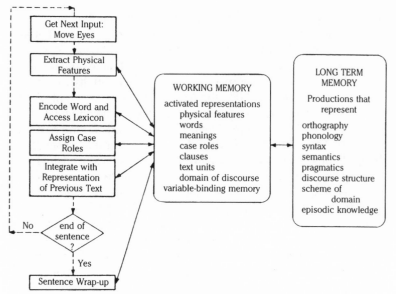

Fig. 4.   Model of the reading process.

that "meaning" is further integrated into long-term memory according to the reader's knowledge of the circumstances surrounding the reading (pragmatics), his knowledge of the discourse structure involved, and his knowledge of the subject. However, Rosenblatt has pointed out that reading research bases models such as this on mechanical or computer systems, which at best describe what she calls "efferent" reading, a kind of reading in which we "carry away" a message.[36] When we read a work of literature, by James or anyone else, we engage the text in a fundamentally different way, according to Rosenblatt: we read for the *experience* of the text in what Rosenblatt calls "aesthetic" reading, and in the process we engage the text with what Eliseo Vivas calls "rapt attention," we experience the text as a "felt presence."[37] Clearly, the assumptions and knowledge we bring to aesthetic reading are somewhat different from those we bring to efferent reading.

Although Rosenblatt's point is well taken, I think that the principles of "selective attention" and "fitting new knowledge into previous knowledge" would seem to apply to any kind of reading, aesthetic or otherwise.[38] We bring to a text, including its style, our knowledge, our memories, our interests, our prejudices and presuppositions—a lesson that Jacques Barzun learned from William James:

Having learned [from reading *The Principles of Psychology*] that perception is fused sensation and thought, surrounded by a fringe of memories and fluid emotions, I realized that in looking at works of art, or hearing or reading them, the object cannot be seen "as it really is," no matter how familiar one may be with the technique of the art or the principles of criticism. The person, the moment, the mood, the past—the apperceptive mass, in short—are inseparable from "the object," as in every experience.[39]

In summary, we cannot equate the words on the page necessarily with the author's intention or with a reader-critic's understanding of them. We can only assert that particular forms of language have a potential for wide and various meanings and that these meanings can be realized only by particular people in particular situations under particular circumstances. In order for us to understand how a particular meaning is realized in a particular situation we need to know both the person who understands the language and the situation in which he did so, as well as the codes, rules, or conventions he was bringing into play during that situation.

Such a view challenges the notion that precise linguistic analysis is more objective than traditional literary criticism. The criticism of Roger Fowler, the most outspoken of the linguistic critics, is marked by a leap from precise textual description to an interpretation of what that description means, an interpretation largely determined ahead of time by Fowler's interests and method of analysis. Fowler presents his interpretation of one passage from *The Ambassadors*, for example, in a very traditional form: he announces the point of his interpretation, he quotes from a "typical" passage, and he gives the passage a "close reading," picking out those features which support his interpretation. The theme of Fowler's interpretation is that James' style "displays the quality of the character's engagement with the world."[40] The "typical" passage from *The Ambassadors* is as follows:

1. She had, this lady, a perfect plain propriety, an expensive subdued suitability, that her companion was not free to analyse, but that struck him, so that his consciousness of it was instantly acute, as a quality quite new to him. 2. Before reaching her he stopped on the grass and went through the form of feeling for something, possibly forgotten, in the light overcoat he carried on his arm; yet the essence of the act was no more than the impulse to gain time. 3. Nothing could have been odder than Strether's

sense of himself as at that moment launched in something of which the sense would be quite disconnected from the sense of his past and which was literally beginning there and then. 4. It had begun in fact already upstairs and before the dressing-glass that struck him as blocking further, so strangely, the dimness of the window of his dull bedroom; begun with a sharper survey of the elements of Appearance than he had for a long time been moved to make. 5. He had during those moments felt these elements to be not so much to his hand as he should have liked, and then had fallen back on the thought that they were precisely a matter as to which help was supposed to come from what he was about to do. 6. He was about to go up to London, so that hat and necktie might wait. 7. What had come as straight to him as a ball in a well-played game—and caught moreover not less neatly—was just the air, in the person of his friend, of having seen and chosen, the air of achieved possession of those vague qualities and quantities that collectively figured to him as the advantage snatched from lucky chances. 8. Without pomp or circumstance, certainly, as her original address to him, equally with his own response, had been, he would have sketched to himself his impression of her as: "Well, she's more thoroughly civilized—!" 9. If "More thoroughly than *whom?*" would not have been for him a sequel to this remark, that was just by reason of his deep consciousness of the bearing of his comparison. (AMB, I, 9)

And the primary data to support Fowler's interpretation are the number of nominalized adjectives or predicates which indicate to Fowler "an alienated psychic universe in which perception, feeling, and personal attributes are shifted outside the subject's active control and away from the center of his personality."[41] Here is the key passage in which Fowler leaps from his description to an interpretation of it:

Typically, any potential action predicates and state predicates which are attached to Strether are nominalized, as, for instance, in the final sentence 9: "sequel," "remark," "consciousness," "bearing," "comparison." Some of these nominalizations are transformations of predicates which might have been realized as verbs—"he remarked"—"his remark"—while others are nominalizations away from adjectives: "he was conscious"—"his consciousness." The substitution of nouns for action verbs, found throughout the passage, is a standard convention in discourse contexts like this, and has obvious connotations of inactivity, repression of the agency function, reduction in the strength of the will in those human characters to whom this style is applied.[42]

It is by no means obvious or objective that nominalizations inherently connote inactivity, repression, and reduction in the strength of the will. They may so connote to Fowler. Whether they do so for us will depend on whether we are persuaded by his argument. I happen to agree that Fowler is on to something, but I think he greatly overstates his case. Those nominalizations do give me a sense of Strether's mental awareness of his surroundings but not that he is inactive or lacking in will. Fowler, I think, is caught up in a metaphor: he takes a grammatical description—nominalization as the repression of agency—and applies it thematically—because Strether's consciousness is described with repressed agents, Strether himself must be somehow repressed in will. This is a fine example of what I mean by "Style as Imitation," which, as I mentioned earlier, I will develop at length in chapter 5. My point here is that Fowler's analysis is not "objective" at all. It is loaded with implicit assumptions and values from the very beginning, and not just in the interpretation of the nominalizations. Of all the possible features to notice in this passage from James, why notice the nominalizations at all? The answer is that Fowler's analysis comes in a section of his book called "Discourse," in which Fowler argues that the language of fiction may indicate a "mind-style" or a "structure of consciousness." This in itself is an assumption that needs to be argued; in fact, the passage from James is part of Fowler's argument that this fundamental assumption is true. The counter argument is equally reasonable and obvious: that language is so conventional and that various ways of expressing something are so limited, the implications of an expression may be simply a convenient convention rather than an indication of an author's subtle intent. It does not matter that Fowler may have started with what he thought to be a neutral attitude (What can I make of this text?), studied the passage, noticed the nominalizations, and tried to discover a reason for them. The very fact that he was writing a book entitled *Linguistics and the Novel*, the fact that he had at his disposal extensive knowledge of linguistics, predisposed him to notice nominalizations over other aspects of the text. Why not notice, for example, sentence length, sentence type, rhetorical tropes, sound patterns, or configurations of letters? Perhaps Fowler did, but sooner or later he had to settle on a focus for his energies, a way of justifying the features he had noticed—the critical act of interpretation. Once Fowler decided upon a rationale for the features he had noticed—in this case, that the style illustrates Strether's passivity—he had to dismiss all the irrelevant data from his argument. And what he was left with is a standard critical interpretation, elegant in form but perfectly circular in argument. James' use of nominalizations expresses Strether's inactivity, but the major evidence we have that Strether is inactive is that James describes him with nominalizations.[43] I do not mean to make fun of Fowler. What he does is often excellent literary criticism, but it is no different in kind from literary criticism as it has always been practiced. Sooner or later, all critics of style, if they want to avoid being trivial, must stop randomly describing a text and start providing a rationale for the features they discover or speculate about the affective impact of those features. And that rationale, that speculation is an interpretation. If the critic does not offer an explicit rationale, then his interpretation is implicit in his choice of features in the first place. That does not make the act of interpretation circular. We study a text until we discover an appropriate interpretation or we denigrate the text because we cannot find one. We do not necessarily find what we have been looking for all along. But the argument we use to present our discovery of an interpretation must of necessity be circular: all we can say about our discovery is that these features of the text led us to it. No other argument is possible.[44]

The act of critical interpretation, then, is very personal, subject to the constraints of particular people in particular situations constructing meaning according to their own background and knowledge and the exigencies of the moment. To a certain extent, of course, our personal interpretations share a large number of assumptions with what Fish has called an interpretive community, but our individual application of those assumptions will be unique to our personal histories and our individual circumstances.[45] It might be helpful to view the relationship between an individual interpretation and the practice of an interpretive community as analogous to the relationship between an individual's ideolect and a community dialect. Features of an individual interpretation will be unique but still share a number of codes, rules, and conventions with a larger critical community.

The fact that interpretations are personal, however, does not mean that criticism is any less important or rigorous than it could otherwise be by claiming some kind of vaunted objectivity. Nor is it solipsistic. We share, after all, a common language, similar neural engineering, and a common reality, however improvised and conventional that shared reality may be. Criticism need not be merely "subjective" or "reader-centered," an exploration of personal identity themes or private associations, as Norman Holland and David Bleich assert.[46] Most of us read criticism because we are interested in literature and what people think about it, not because we are interested in the mental history and emotional life of the critic. Nevertheless, it is extremely difficult to separate the two.

Traditional criticism has compounded the difficulty by evolving a vocabulary for treating literature as an objective phenomenon that is just as misleading as the claims for objectivity by the linguists. Traditional critics use the universal "we" to refer to a common experience of literature, they talk about the "effects" which literature produces in readers, they discuss "expectations and satisfactions" in a text, as if these things also applied to all readers. Once upon a time, it may have been understood, albeit unconsciously, that these terms were metaphorical ways of talking about an abstract interpretive thesis, a hypothetical case of how someone, not even the critic using the words, might understand a text or interact with it. Despite their use of this terminology, traditional critics rarely offer their own introspective versions of how they actually read the text and its emotional impact at the time of the reading. In traditional criticism such information was and still is considered irrelevant.[47] But with the advent of reader-response criticism and renewed interest in the "ontological status" of literary art, such terminology can be very misleading, especially when it is combined with a theory of reading that attempts to outline in broad terms how readers as a class in fact comprehend texts, which is what many reader-response critics try to do. I think we can bridge the gap between "personal" biographical interpretations and more conventional interpretations. Indeed, I think we need both kinds of criticism if we are to understand fully how we read literature. But in order to bridge the gap, we need to clarify what *kind* of interpretation we are engaged in: we need to make as explicit as possible the rules and conventions we want to formalize as a procedure in explaining a text, the rules and conventions in play in any particular interpretation. To be this explicit we need to make a number of distinctions.

Up until now I have been using *interpretation* in the sense of a critical or scholarly activity one step removed from the act of taking in the meaning of the words on the page, a process that George Dillon describes as taking place in three steps: perception, comprehension, and interpretation. According to Dillon, in perception we as readers specify to ourselves the propositional structure of the text, in comprehension we integrate the propositions into a "running tally of what is being described or argued in the passage," and in interpretation "we relate the sense of what is going on to the author's constructive intention—why he is saying what he says, or what he is getting at in terms of the themes and meaning of his work."[48] Although Dillon argues that interpretation can "shape" perception and comprehension, he is using the term *interpretation* differently from the way I have been using it. Dillon uses the term to refer to a part of the process of reading, of getting meaning from the page. That is a meaning of *interpretation* which in traditional criticism encompasses the process of understanding how a particular episode of a novel describes a character or advances the plot or even how a passage relates to larger thematic concerns. In phenomenological terms this level of interpretation is similar to Rosenblatt's term *evocation* or Ingarden's and Iser's term *concretization* of the literary text; it is the process by which a text is perceived, attended to, internalized by the reader.

However, justifying the particular grammatical or rhetorical forms of a passage, or in more traditional criticism, relating a particular work to its social milieu or any larger critical framework, seems to go one step beyond *evocation* or *concretization* (or *interpretation* in Dillon's sense). *Interpretation* as I have been using the term is not concerned with local "meanings" but with relating particular features of the text to a more abstract or theoretical system. I can understand the meaning of *The Ambassadors*, or of particular passages in *The Ambassadors*, without ever having noticed, at least consciously, that the prose is heavy with nominalizations or passive constructions or that it reflects the growing subjectivity of late-nineteenth-century fiction. I think it important, then, to distinguish between *interpretation* as part of the process of reading, as *evocation* or *concretization*, and *interpretation* as a much more abstract or theoretical activity, which is almost inevitably a result of rereading or hypothetically reconstructing how we read the text the first time, of applying a frame of reference and discerning the relevant codes and conventions in our evocation or concretization.[49]

Distinguishing between these two kinds of interpretation is crucial because of the widely held assumption in literary criticism that the text shapes the way we read it, that the way we take in the meaning of the passage determines how we think of it in a broader critical framework. In its simplest, most popular form this assumption is that the fact of a text, its particular diction and syntax, can be taken as evidence of how we read it and the effects it creates in us. In practice, this means that the critic does not have to discuss actual effects, the only evidence of which is introspection about his own reading or the reports of others. All the critic has to do is cite certain features of the text, which in and of themselves are offered as evidence of the effects they cause. Fowler, for example, assumes the connection between stylistic features and the effects they cause quite explicitly:

> [The author] can assume that a responsible reading, at least by a contemporary, will retrieve surface structure in very much the form that he, the writer, arranged it; and that surface structure can thus be deployed to determine the perception of particular textual significances. These possibilities for the control of decoding follow from the extent to which linguistic competence (contrasted with competence in other semiological systems) is shared among the members of a community. It seems to follow that the structure of language as the reader experiences it—that is, the text's overt or surface structure—is a fundamental and indispensible object of study for the analyst of text structure. This principle is in fact so well established in stylistics (if not in the generative framework) that I will offer no further justification.[50]

Fowler's principle may be well established in linguistics and literary criticism in general, but that does not mean the principle has an adequate justification. Talbot Taylor has argued convincingly that the assumption of common stylistic effects is based on a faulty analogy with linguistic competence. Just because we share a common language structure, a common means of perceiving and understanding that language, and therefore, in some sense, a shared understanding of the content of any given form of language—what linguists and psychologists call inter-subjectivity—it does not follow that we also share a common perceptual or emotional affect.[51] Readers may be able to agree on the words of a text (although even establishing the words of a text involves interpretive assumptions and procedures), but they will not agree on which words are most important and ought to be paid attention to, to say nothing of what the words mean and the affects they cause.[52] The history of interpretive responses to, say, "The Turn of the Screw" is a history of how words, phrases, and larger passages affect different critics in entirely different ways, even if they do agree to focus on the same features of the text.[53]

We know from reading research that readers do not necessarily follow syntax word for word in the order in which they occur on the page, that even if they do, they may not relate what they read into comparable presuppositions or bases of knowledge, that therefore there may be little or no correlation between a given set of features on the page and the order and method with which it is perceived by various readers. The latest theories of reading relate *evocation* or *concretization* to very broad strategies for reading, and these strategies are usually semantically based, a way of integrating our comprehension of individual words, phrases, and sentences into larger frames of reference and bases of knowledge. Thomas Bever, a noted linguist and cognitive psychologist, describes the process of comprehending sentences this way:

> In the actual application of language, specific contexts must provide far stronger immediate constraints and basis for prediction of the most likely meaning of a sentence independent of its form. Thus, most normal perceptual processing of sentences is probably carried out with little regard to actual sequence or structure; rather, the basic relational functions (actor, action, object-modifier) are assigned on the basis of temporary ('contingent') and generic ('constant') semantic probabilities.[54]

Readers must fit these "relational functions" into larger bases of knowledge—schemata—according to their intentions and goals, their focus and attention as they read. And this selective attention, this fit of perception to previous knowledge, is unique from reader to reader.

Despite the general consensus among reading researchers that a great deal of the meaning we get from a text depends upon what we as readers bring to the page, many literary critics continue to argue as if there were some common psychological effects inherent in our perception of certain textual features. Thus, for example, David Lodge asserts that the image of the boat in book 8 of *The Ambassadors*, based as it is, according to Lodge, on the expression "in the same boat," is an example of a "startling concreteness of elaboration." Here is the passage Lodge is referring to:

> As she thus publicly drew him into her boat she produced in him such a silent agitation as he was not to fail afterwards to denounce as pusillanimous . . . . It would be exactly *like* the way things always turned out for him that he should affect Mrs. Pocock and Waymarsh as launched in a relation in which he had really never been launched at all. There were at this very moment—they could only be—attributing to him the full license

of it and all by the operation of her own tone with him; whereas
his sole license had been to cling with intensity to the brink, not
to dip so much as toe into the flood. But the flicker of his fear on
this occasion was not, as may be added, to repeat itself; it sprang
up, for its moment, only to die down and then go out forever. To
meet his fellow visitor's invocation and, with Sarah's brilliant eyes
upon him, answer, *was* quite sufficiently to step into her boat.
During the rest of the time her visit lasted he felt himself proceed
to each of the proper offices, successively, for helping to keep the
adventurous skiff afloat. It rocked beneath him, but he settled
himself in his place. He took up an oar and, since he was to have
the credit of pulling, pulled. (AMB, II, 94–95)

Lodge comments: "The effect is rather like that of the heroic simile in
epic poetry, where the 'tenor' recedes from sight, and the 'vehicle' takes
on an independent poetic life."[55] Now, when I first read this passage
the similarity to a heroic simile did not occur to me. Indeed, it never
dawned on me that James may be playing with the notion of "in the
same boat." The idea still seems to me a little far-fetched. In any case,
I think I understand what Lodge is referring to: he is commenting on
James' occasional use of an extended metaphor and the way such a
metaphor may distance us from the action James is describing. Whether
James' elaborate metaphor literally affects me in the same way as a
heroic simile, I cannot tell. I was not aware of how the passage affected
me at all during my first reading. As a metaphor for a description of
how the passage may hypothetically work, I can accept Lodge's description. My immediate point, however, is that the words on the page
cannot necessarily be used as evidence for how they affect me. I could
argue against Lodge, as many critics do for Jamesian devices, that the
elaborate metaphor ought to involve the reader more intimately with
the objects and actions described by the text because the sheer elab-
orateness of the metaphor requires the reader to dedicate himself to
working out what the metaphor refers to. To settle the difference in
effect, we can only appeal to our experience of the text, and at least
in my case, I am not sure which explanation does account for how I
originally read the passage.

Thus when we assert in stylistic criticism that a given stylistic feature
has a certain "effect" or a particular meaning, we need to make clear
the rules or conventions with which we are using these terms: we need
to indicate whether we are using the term *effect* literally or metaphorically, as a statement about how we actually reacted to a text, as a

hypothetical statement about how anyone could possibly react (a claim about the reading process in general), or as a metaphoric way of talking about a particular insight we have had. The rules of evidence will be entirely different, depending on which *effect* we are referring to.

If we use the term *effect* literally we may be referring to what we immediately perceive or comprehend or emotionally react to: your grasping the sense of what I am saying right now, for example. In certain situations our comprehension may be accompanied by an overt emotional response—breaking out in tears at bad news, puzzlement at obscurities, laughter at jokes—or our comprehension may be accompanied by a range of associations and other mental activities. This kind of effect, the subjective response to the text, is the effect that David Bleich and Norman Holland suggest ought to be the basis of criticism. And it may be this kind of effect that accounts for the reaction to James' late style that it is dense or forbidding.

After some reflection or upon rereading a text, however, we may be affected differently—just as we may come out of a meeting with our boss and spend the rest of the day recalling it, mulling it over, wondering whether we said the right thing and pondering the implications of certain things the boss said, the implications of certain expressions on his face. What such a situation means to us, the effect it has on us, may change the more we think about it. If we decide that the boss may not have been as hostile as we originally thought, we may be reassured, and thus, this second kind of effect may also have an emotional side. In thinking about literature we may realize certain things in the text that we missed during our first reading or make certain associations we did not make at first. In my experience rereading and further thinking rarely produce an emotional response to the text itself, although I may feel the joy of discovering something I had previously overlooked, or I may come to regard the text more favorably or unfavorably. When we speak of *effect* in the sense of an immediate emotional or perceptual response or in the sense of what we discovered upon rereading or further thinking, we are using the word quite literally to refer to our actual responses to the text, as best we know them. Such responses, it seems to me, can be used as perfectly good evidence of what a text can mean, but in noting such responses the reader-critic needs to perform the complicated job of monitoring his own responses as closely as possible *while* he is reading or do so under the control of some kind of experimental procedure which would provide the necessary conventions for interpreting the response. The reason for taking such care is that certain kinds of intuition and introspection are notoriously unreliable. The most reliable kind of self-reflection about reading is based on *recent, focused* recollections of reading: recollections which may still be, or recently were, in short-term memory, and which are focused on what happened during the reading process as such rather than on inferences or generalizations about the reading process.[56] The further a reader-critic is from the moment of reading he is trying to monitor, the more his responses will be colored by previous assumptions and larger theoretical rationales. A large number of experiments in psychology have demonstrated that people tend to offer rationales for their behavior which are quite different from the causes indicated by the experiments that elicited their behavior in the first place.[57] This is not to say that recent and focused introspection about the act of reading is unaffected by previous assumptions and knowledge. It is only to say that the reader-critic has a better chance of achieving insight into how he reads if his introspection is under some kind of experimental control (such as what psychologists call a stimulated recall interview) or if his introspection is as close as possible to the act of reading and his avowed purpose is to monitor his own reading rather than to recall it later. Relevant to such "case studies" of the reading process are all of the circumstances under which the reader is attending to the text. Such introspective accounts will be just as controlled by some governing codes, rules, and conventions as more traditional interpretations; the problem is to make these codes and conventions explicit, either in the form of the experiment or in the way a single critic attempts to monitor his own responses.

The question, of course, is the degree to which even the most reliable introspection can uncover or capture the underlying mental processes involved in reading. If we do rely on introspective accounts, in what sense are they reliable? Are they only constructs, another text to decode? Are they tips of the iceberg, suggestive but fragmentary and incomplete? Are they sufficiently reliable to base a theory of reading on—or even a single interpretation?[58] In answer to such questions, I would say, once again, that it depends: it depends on what the introspection reveals about reading and the claims which the critic makes for his insights. In any case, I think that introspective accounts of the effects of texts can be offered as evidence of a claim about what the text means or how it works as long as we are sure of the kind of claim that the critic is making.

But the more we study a text under the assumption that the text is inherently meaningful and the more we are intent on finding something—a new angle, a relationship between two things we had not considered before—the more we try to apply our personal associations or a specific critical concept—plot formats, syntactic patterning, allusions—the more, in short, we try to discover significance, the more we will find. And when we talk about what we have found, we often of necessity must speak metaphorically, describing our discovery in terms of how various things may have affected us unconsciously during our first reading or in terms of the intention of the writer. I recall the moment during a rereading of *The Ambassadors* when I suddenly realized that Chad and Madame de Vionnet are often absent from Paris at the same time, and I immediately wondered why Strether did not notice it, too. I automatically assumed that their absence was intentional, that James was using this device to dramatize how uncomprehending Strether is or to distance the reader from Strether by pointing out his lack of perception. My attempt to explain the source of my discovery is precisely where the limits of critical language begin. Of course, I have no evidence other than the text for what James originally intended and as for whether the absence of the lovers distances the reader from Strether, I can only offer my own experience. On my first reading of the novel I did not even notice the absence of the lovers, and upon rereading and discovering the fact, I was less aware of being distanced from Strether than I was aware that being distanced from Strether was a way of explaining the absence of the lovers. In short, the effect of distancing was entirely hypothetical, a way of accounting for what I discovered in the text by the conventions of a critical method, and as far as I know, it had no overt relation to an actual effect on me at all. If the absence of the lovers *did* have an effect on me, it was entirely subliminal or quickly forgotten. The conventions of a certain critical procedure determined how I thought of and interpreted my discovery.

So it is with most of our discoveries based upon a close reading of subtle wording in the text. Our ability to explain them is limited to conventional hypotheses about authorial intention or the effect on readers. Neither hypothesis can be demonstrated as being literally true. Reader-response critics try to relate personal experiences and reactions to the text as much as possible to a hypothetical case of what they were experiencing as they read, but in many cases their reconstructions of the process are so far removed from immediate recollection that their hypotheses are no closer to the act of reading than those of traditional critics who try to frame their hypotheses in terms of theme or character. Both reader-response and traditional criticism most often use metaphors, either to the act of reading or to a hypothetical intention embodied in the text.

The distinction between literal and metaphorical effects becomes crucial when we use certain metaphors which seem to be based on an empirical reality but which are entirely hypothetical, unrelated to anyone's experience of the text or a possible intention. One such claim common in Jamesian criticism is that James' prose "creates its own readers," that we somehow read James' late style in a qualitatively different way than we read other styles, that syntax is a metaphor for how we read it. Here are a few examples:

Evidently [James'] use of pronouns implies a demand on the Reader's attention: he must remember what the pronoun stands for, or rather (for no one will consent to such repeated effort where only amusement is at stake) the Reader will have to be, spontaneously, at full cock of attention, a person accustomed to bear things in mind, to carry on a meaning from sentence to sentence, to think in abbreviations; in other words he will have to be an intellectual, as distinguished from an impulsive or *imageful*, person.[59]

One might add [to Vernon Lee's comments quoted above] that the use of personal pronouns instead of proper names heightens the sense of intimacy and intense engagement with the characters, draws the reader closer to them, more completely into their network of relations.[60]

In following the progress of meaning through the sentence, the reader must keep its beginning in mind through to the end, suspending judgment like the delayed and interrupted action of the sentence itself, until, as Vernon Lee makes clear, all this "holding back merely hurls meaning along with accumulated force" . . . James' arrangement of these word groups [clauses within clauses] requires the reader to follow several syntactical patterns collecting meaning as he goes.[61]

Mystery occurs, then, not because Strether's specific thoughts are themselves inscrutable, but because James knows that he can successfully create the illusion of Strether thinking only if he can generate an analogous process in us. The very presence of an initial metaphor or negation will impel us farther into the passage for elucidation. The eventual literal or positive statement does not in turn function as a simple authorial explanation. We escape our initial puzzlement only by joining the metaphor and the literal or negative and positive elements together in our minds. Our minds are made to move, to jump like a spark across a dark gap. We ourselves create that relationship, that connection, which is meaning.[62]

There is a fine line between metaphoric attempts to explain the effects of James' prose and certain hypotheses which are beyond our ability to affirm or deny them, and it seems to me that the claims I have just cited cross that line. To begin with, I am not at all certain how literally to take these claims: I do not know what codes, rules, or conventions are being used. As I have already argued, we have little evidence that all readers follow syntax word for word in the same way "collecting meaning as they go" or that "our minds are made to move" in the same way when we read the same passage. If these claims are literal, the critics making them are not offering their experience or anyone else's as evidence that they are true. I think it more likely these claims are metaphoric. But even if they are, I know of no way to judge their appropriateness, since as far as I know there is no reason to think that James' prose causes us to pay more attention to pronoun reference or the precise form of his sentences than any other kind of prose. All pronouns cause us to "bear things in mind" and to "carry on a meaning from sentence to sentence." All sentences force us to keep their "beginning in mind through to the end." All prose causes our minds to move to "create that relationship, that connection, which is meaning." James may use more pronouns than other writers, he may use longer and more complicated sentences than other writers, but it does not follow that when we read James' prose "our minds are made to move" in a qualitatively different way from the way we read any prose. Even George Dillon in his study of the ways in which readers may "process" James' prose—as well as the prose of four other writers—assumes that the same basic "processing strategies" adopted by various readers will apply to all five writers and that the strategies may be applied differently by different readers. The only necessary connection Dillon makes between syntax and a particular way of reading that syntax is negative; that is, the way we read a given passage must not be contradicted by its syntax.[63] In short, it seems to me that the claim that James' prose creates its own readers is just the kind of blurring of the literal and the metaphoric, the actual and the hypothetical, which results in criticism beyond the bounds of either the literal or the metaphoric. We have no way of judging the appropriateness of the metaphor since the 'vehicle' itself is hypothetical, and we have no evidence for the literal assertion, either. This blurring of the literal and the metaphoric is most common in arguments about hypothetical readers: "implied readers," "informed readers," and others. The evidence for such readers is overwhelmingly in the text, usually in the syntax but also in larger units of discourse, not in the reading process as such, so that a model of reading becomes a metaphoric way of justifying a particular interpretation. This kind of interpretive procedure, making the language of the text a metaphor for a mental process, is one example of what I call Style as Imitation, and I discuss similar kinds of metaphors for mental process in chapter 5.

Perhaps it seems like common sense to argue that our insights about James are not just insights but indications of something more—of the way we read and think or the way everyone reads and thinks. After all, the leap backwards from what we think to how we must have thought it seems at first glance to be perfectly reasonable. But it is not. The ways of the mind are intricate and complex, and there is no logical or necessary reason why *what* we think must mirror or in any way capture the *way* we think. The claims of what we think and how we think are entirely different.

Thus it seems to me that we need to distinguish the kinds of claims we make about effects and also make clear the kinds of evidence we must cite to support such claims: we must make clear the codes, rules, or conventions that are governing our interpretations. Certain kinds of effects, such as those in response to a first reading, or even of a rereading, can be documented only by personal experience or case studies of the way particular readers in fact read the text. Such studies are most reliable when they report the results of introspection during or shortly after reading, when the subjects infer or generalize as little as possible about the process. To support claims about the effects of subsequent readings or the way in which the text fits into a broader theoretical framework, we must of necessity speak metaphorically, although such claims may be literal if they are talking about later cognitive realizations and not our perceptions and emotions while we were reading the first time. In subsequent chapters I will try to spell out a number of ways to make such claims more explicit.

The interplay of codes, rules, and conventions in the way we interpret makes "truth" and "reality" very pragmatic. Our simplest perceptions are conditioned in ways we are barely aware of.[64] The more we make such conventions explicit, the more we realize how little we know ourselves and what causes us to read in a particular way. Our best interpretations and theories are often mere conjectures; they are often playful explorations of what things may mean or what they can mean, flirtations with possibilities—or with nonsense. A particular critical insight of mine, an interpretation, a theory of reading, may eventually prove unhelpful or implausible to most readers or it may even be outside the realm of possibility in a more reliable empirical theory of reading. Nevertheless, I continue to interpret, speculate, theorize: What do these words mean to me? What could these words mean to me? What could these words mean to anyone? In what sense? For what reasons? And the only constraints on my interpretations, my speculations, and my theories are the conventions I can discover to bring into play, my ability to formalize them, and my ability to persuade others that they are worth considering.

In criticism, as in literature, we need to extend language to the limits of its possible meanings, to what Marvin Bell calls its nonsensical end, because only there can we grapple with the importance and impact of literature: "yet there is safety only there." But in our investigation of "why Mr. Henry James wrote that way," it would not hurt to also investigate why we write the way we do in talking about James, so that like James' prose our critical language can go "out with the tide, but further." That is what I propose to do now—investigate the ways we have extended the limits of critical language in order to come to grips with the language of Henry James.

3. *Style as Identification*

The late style is, of course, *sui generis,* and uniformly so: all of James's fiction after, say, 1900 immediately identifies itself as Jamesian.

—Leo Hendrick

The weather had changed, the rain was ugly, the wind was wicked, the sea impossible, *because* of Lord Mark. It was because of him, *a fortiori,* that the palace was closed. Densher went round again twice, and found the visitor each time as he had found him first. Once, that is, he was staring before him; the next time he was looking over his *Figaro,* which he had opened out. Densher didn't again stop, but he left him apparently unconscious of his passage—on another repetition of which Lord Mark had disappeared. He had spent but the day; he would be off that night; he had now gone to his hotel for arrangements. These things were as plain to Densher as if he had had them in words. The obscure had cleared for him—if cleared it was; there was something he didn't see, the great thing; but he saw so round it and so close to it that this was almost as good.

—Henry James

The passage above was written by Henry James in the winter of 1901–2 at the height of his "late manner": it occurs in the thirtieth chapter of *The Wings of the Dove.* The striking thing about the passage, of course, is that despite Leo Hendrick's assertion it does not sound like James, and I suspect that no one familiar with James but unfamiliar with *The Wings of the Dove* would readily identify the passage as Jamesian or be able to pick it out of a number of anonymous passages of late Victorian or Edwardian prose, such as is required of some advanced students of English on final tests and comprehensive examinations. I asserted earlier that despite different definitions and theories of style we all recognize what we are referring to when we talk of James's late style—or when we talk of any style, for that matter. While I still think the assertion is true, I think so for vastly different reasons from most theorists of style. As that description of Densher's vigil from *The Wings of the Dove* demonstrates, James often did not write like James—and for very good reasons. Most writers do not, indeed cannot, write like themselves for very long. The forms of language are too conventional, and a great deal of the language we use is limited by the conventions of various rhetorical situations. Carl Klaus has pointed out the difficulties in identifying an author with a particular style, but his wisdom has been ignored. Klaus cites four radically different passages:

> About this time I met with an odd volume of *The Spectator*. It was the third. I had never before seen any of them. I bought it, read it over and over, and was much delighted with it. I thought the writing excellent, and wished, if possible, to imitate it. Forasmuch as the enemies of America, in the Parliament of Great Britain, to render us odious to the nation, and give an ill impression of us in the minds of other European powers, have represented us as unjust and ungrateful in the highest degree; asserting on every occasion, that the colonies were settled at the expence of Britain; that they were, at the expence of the same, protected in their infancy; that they now ungratefully and unjustly refuse to contribute to their own protection . . .

> There is in every village a vacant dwelling, called the strangers' house. Here they are placed, while the old men go round from hut to hut, acquainting the inhabitants, that strangers are arrived, who are probably hungry and weary; and every one sends them what he can spare of victuals, and skins to repose on.

> Be studious in your profession, and you will be learned. Be industrious and frugal, and you will be rich. Be sober and temperate, and you will be healthy. Be in general virtuous, and you will be happy.[1]

Each of these passages was written by one man—Benjamin Franklin. Klaus goes on to discuss the implications of one man writing in such a wide variety of styles:

Given four passages so different in style, one could hardly believe they were written by a single man, and yet they were. All are by Benjamin Franklin.

In view of this perplexing situation, one might well be moved to ask which one of these styles *is* the man; and the answer of course would be that all of these styles are the man, the corollary of which is that no single one of them fully represents Franklin, that none of these styles is the man. Each of them is in a sense an invention of Franklin, a fictional personality he creates to meet the needs of a different purpose, audience, or occasion. . . . Tentatively, then, we might say that style is the result of a complex set of mental activities, beginning within the man, moving out to the world, as private purposes become shaped by the exigencies of public communication, and returning once again to the man, when the writer chooses the precise form in which to accommodate himself to the world and its conventions.[2]

Even if we restrict our attention to an author's work in a single genre—to James' fiction, for example—we will find a wide range of individual features or "substyles" that do not fit into our conception of the author's style as a whole. Once again, the problem is one of defining how we are using a term that is used to refer to a wide variety of concepts and meanings, and once again, I think it would be more useful to think of style as a function of a particular reader-critic's perception of the text or of his purposes and critical procedures than as a series of features inherent in the text.

Let us look, first of all, at a number of features which various critics have identified as being typical of James' fiction:

1. The use of intangible nouns as the subjects of sentences, nouns such as "analogy," "elements," "impression," as well as such noun clauses as "what was clear" and "what impressed him."
2. Deictic pronouns as the subjects of sentences, pronouns such as "it," "they," "one," and "another," as well as such pointers as "the matter," "the former," "the latter," and "a great deal."
3. The use of "it" or "there" as a head word or expletive.
4. Placing active agents in "oblique" grammatical positions, as in "These things were early signs in him that . . . ."

5. The use of verbs of mental action, verbs such as "notice," "perceive," "feel," "believe," and "have the sense of," as well as certain "recipient" forms: "be definite to," "bring home to," "strike," and "present itself to."
6. The use of past perfect tenses.
7. The use of "loose" sentences with "weak" conjunctions: "He prolonged it a little, in the immediate neighborhood, after he had quitted his chair; and the upshot of the whole morning for him was that his campaign had begun."
8. The use of semi-colons to signal loosely attached participials or supplemental phrases or clauses: "It was at this point, however, that she remained; changing her place, moving from the shabby sofa to the armchair upholstered in a glazed cloth that gave at once—she had tried it—the sense of the slippery and of the sticky."
9. Parenthetical interruptions at odd places: "But anything like his actual state had not, as to the prohibition of impulse, accident, range—the prohibition, in other words, of freedom—hitherto known."
10. The use of ambiguous conditionals: "If she continued to wait it was really in a manner that she mightn't add the shame of fear, of individual, of personal collapse, to all the other shames." This is not a standard contrary-to-fact if-clause: Millie is in fact continuing to wait. Dillon calls this usage "an odd sort of concessive conjunct ("if x is so [and though somewhat unexpected, it does seem to be so], then it is less unexpected when we consider y")."[3]
11. The use of logical terms, such as "law," "theory," and "relation."
12. The use of colloquial two-word verbs: "have out with," "take in," "pull in," "have in," and "cast about."
13. The use of italicized words for emphasis, especially words of relationship in dialogue: "What in the world is he *to* us?"

Linguistic critics document their characterizations of James' late style by citing statistics on how often features such as these recur in selected passages of James' novels and stories, often in comparison with fiction by other authors. Thus, for example, Seymour Chatman asserts that *it* as an expletive is typical of James' fictional prose because in a selected passage from *The Wings of the Dove* that form occurs as the subject of main clauses 8 percent of the time, while in comparable passages by Forster, Gissing, Butler, and Conrad, *it* as an expletive only occurs as the subject of main clauses from 1 to 5 percent of the time.[4] Another common way in which linguistic critics characterize the late style is by comparing it with James' early work. Thus, for example, Leo Hendrick asserts that James' late style is more complex than his earlier style (from 1865 to 1877) because in 400 sample sentences from each period James' use of complex and compound-complex sentences rose from an average of 6.5 and 5.7 sentences out of every 20 sentences in the early style to 8.1 and 7.9 sentences out of every 20 in the late style. At the same time James' use of simple and compound sentences dropped from 4.5 and 3.2 sentences out of every 20 sentences in the early style to 1.7 and 2.3 in the late style.[5]

I find such linguistic analyses fascinating, but I think we need to be careful about the conclusions we draw from them. Above all, we need to affirm that such studies do *not* give us an "objective" picture of what James' style is "really" like. For one thing, statistical and comparative studies do not pretend to describe any given passage of Jamesian prose. They present a hypothetical model of the prose based on random samples of extended passages. Just as the subjective impressions of a literary critic are determined by his own presuppositions and interests, so too are the results of statistical and comparative studies determined by the presuppositions and interests of the critics conducting them, and as such they are subject to the same objections as the most subjective impressions of James' work. That is, why notice such features as expletives and sentence types in the first place? Why are expletives a significant feature if they are so uncommon? Why should a feature have to recur to be significant at all? How do we explain anomalies, certain passages that do not fit the model? The answer to this last question, of course, is that statistical-comparative studies are not concerned with particular passages; they are concerned with averages, a hypothetical model. They are, in short, useful primarily in relation to the ultimate purpose for which they were originally designed, and that purpose was to identify unknown texts. If we do not know who wrote a novel, ascertaining the statistical features of the text as a whole may help us to relate the text to works with similar features by a known writer and thereby provide us with the identity of the author. In James' case, however, the identity of the work is not in question. We all know who wrote *The Ambassadors, The Wings of the Dove,* and *The Golden Bowl,* and therefore, the use of the statistical-comparative method is deprived of its primary rationale.[6] Why bother to identify the author of a text when we already know who the author is? The alternative rationale most often cited by linguistic critics for the statistical-comparative method is that it can document the "subjective" impressions of others. But that is precisely what the statistical-comparative method cannot do.

Consider for a moment how we as readers and critics come to recognize a distinctive style is the first place. Unless we read a stylistic analysis of the author in question, the only way we can do so is by reading a considerable amount of the author's work and building up what James would call an "impression," a concept of what elements seem most common or distinctive in the style. Our concept of the style must of necessity be determined by our past experience and our present interests, and unless we are a stylistic critic closely analyzing the diction and syntax of the text, we will probably notice only those features which contribute or detract from our ability to read the text, passages of particular eloquence and power, passages which distract and confuse us. I have yet to hear of anyone who finished reading a work by James and exclaimed, "By God, he uses a lot of expletives." Nevertheless, if we are impressed or confused, we may reflect on the text at times and try to discover the source of our reaction, or we may notice that the author seems to express himself with some consistency and we may begin to look for the source of that consistency. The final concept we arrive at will not only be influenced by how often certain features occur but also by individual features that impressed us as we read, and these may not be common at all. They may be determined entirely by our selective attention and the significance we attach to certain details. We build up, in short, a "logical-construct," a hypothetical concept of the style that is entirely determined by our attention, our experience, and the meaning we derive from the text. Our concept of style then will include not only those features which occur again and again but also those which seem significant to us even though they may, at least theoretically, occur only once.

There are, it seems to me, at least three kinds of stylistic features which we may notice for reasons that have nothing to do with how often they occur. First of all, we may be struck by the sheer oddity of a certain expression. For example, every once in a while James breaks up a phrase or a clause that we usually think of as a unit: into this unit he inserts adverbials and appositions of some length, occasionally even parenthetically interrupting his insertion. Usually we keep auxiliaries and main verbs close together; if we do break them up it is most often with only an adverb or two. James, however, is capable of a sentence such as this: "What finally prevailed with him was the reflexion that, whatever might happen, the great man had, after that occasion at the palace, their young woman's brief sacrifice to society—and the hour of Mrs. Stringham's appeal had brought it well to the surface—shown him marked benevolence" (WOD, II, 295–96). James can also do the same thing with dialogue. Into a two-word verb or a similar expression that takes its meaning as a unit he inserts a transition or a colloquial expression. Here are two examples from *The Golden Bowl:* "Giving myself, in other words, away—and perfectly willing to do it for nothing" (GB, I, 98). "She's not selfish—God forgive her!—enough" (GB, I, 101). I know of no studies which document how often James does this sort of thing, but even if he had done so only once, it would be odd and if we noticed it, it would become part of our concept of his style. So, too, with certain features which James uses more consistently. It is my impression that James tends to end units of discourse—paragraphs, sections, and chapters—with "clinchers," dramatic images in simple sentences or periodic sentences which build to a climax and provide us with a hint of what is going to happen next. Here are a few examples from various sources:

Such were the data Basil French's enquiry would elicit: her own six engagements and her mother's three nullified marriages—nine nice distinct little horrors in all. What on earth was to be done about them? ("Julia Bride," end of section 1)

Then harder presses still, sick with the force of his shock, and falling back as under the hot breath and the roused passion of a life larger than his own, a rage of personality before which his own collapsed, he felt the whole vision turn to darkness and his very feet give way. His head went round; he was going; he had gone. ("The Jolly Corner," end of section 2)

She might, for that matter, herself have liked it [Herbert's bow], since, receding further, only with her white face toward him, she paid it the homage of submission. He remained dignified, and she almost humbly went. ("The Bench of Desolation," end of section 4)

She [Maggie] watcher her [Charlotte], splendid and erect, float down the long vista; then she sank upon a seat. Yes, she had done all. (*The Golden Bowl,* end of book 5)

It is not the frequency of these features which makes them so note-worthy but their distribution. To R. W. Short the typical Jamesian sentence may be 35.3 words long and be characterized by loose con-junctions, but such a general hypothetical notion of style tells us very little about how James actually uses sentences.

Finally, James uses certain devices which are dramatically effec-tive—the elaborate patterning of intense moments, an extended me-taphor or the presentation of images in the order in which they are perceived by a central character. Most of the passages cited by critics as examples of James' late style at its best are of this kind—the rec-ognition scene in *The Ambassadors,* the elaborate metaphor of the pagoda which opens book 4 of *The Golden Bowl,* any number of passages in which a character is in intense thought (I am especially fond of the last section of "The Beast in the Jungle."). These passages are important for reasons other than style; they come at moments we find crucial in the novels and stories in question. We find that the prose is heightened, and we pay more attention to the language at these moments because we sense that the language seems inherently more important than at other times, what Bruce Philip Tracy has called, in reference to various meditation scenes "a complex of devices which always reached peak intensity."[7] Just what makes a passage crucial, just what makes the language at a particular point in a novel seem more important than at other times is, of course, entirely a matter of personal discrimination and judgment, the result of how we have read the text up to that point, and our individual concepts of James' style will be determined by the passages we choose to think of as most crucial, passages in which the language seems most important. As I've said, one of my favorite passages is the end of "The Beast in the Jungle." In the final section of that story James intensifies his metaphor of the beast as a sign of Marcher's destiny:

> Her spoken words came back to him—the chain stretched and stretched. The Beast had lurked indeed, and the Beast, at its hour, had sprung; it had sprung in the twilight of the cold April when, pale, ill, wasted, but all beautiful, and perhaps even then recoverable, she had risen from her chair to stand before him and let him imaginably guess. It had sprung as he didn't guess; it had sprung as she hopelessly turned from him, and the mark, by the time he left her, had fallen where it *was* to fall. . . . But the bitterness suddenly sickened him, and it was as if, horribly, he saw, in the truth, in the cruelty of his image, what had been

appointed and done. He saw the Jungle of his life and saw the lurking Beast; then, while he looked, perceived it, as by a stir of the air, rise, huge and hideous, for the leap that was to settle him. His eyes darkened—it was close; and, instinctively turning, in his hallucination, to avoid it, he flung himself, face down, on the tomb. (BIJ, 402)

Rather incongruously, however, James also uses the image of the desert in the story to describe Marcher's mental state, so that the jungle of life and the beast of destiny encroach on the desert of consciousness:

It had always had its incalculable moments of glaring out, quite as with the very eyes of the very Beast, and, used as he was to them, they could still draw from him the tribute of a sigh that rose from the depths of his being. . . . Even his original fear, if fear it had been, had lost itself in the desert. (BIJ, 372)

He had lived, in spite of himself, into his change of feeling, and in wandering over the earth had wandered, as might be said, from the circumference to the centre of his desert. (BIJ, 396–7)

I know of no other story in which James juggles such conflicting metaphors. This one instance is certainly not his common practice, and yet it is an integral part of my concept of James' style, perhaps because it is indicative of something I do associate with James more generally—the boldness, even the outrageousness of his later metaphors. In any case, my point is that our individual concepts of style are determined by our recognition of such passages as the end of "The Beast in the Jungle," and our recognition of such passages—our determining what makes them significant—is a far more complex process than simply noting how often a certain characteristic occurs. When I think of James, certain passages such as the end of "The Beast" immediately come to mind and shape my perception and concept of James' style. I have no idea whether these passages are representative or average; in a sense whether they are representative or average does not matter. I will always associate James with the features of these passages, even if a statistical-comparative study should document beyond a doubt that they are aberrations, total exceptions to the general tone of James' late work.

If our individual concept of style is a kind of hypothetical ideal, a composite of all the different aspects of the style which we have noticed—say, for example, the thirteen features I listed earlier—it follows that no particular passage from an author will contain all thirteen features. Various passages will contain any number of the features in different combinations, and the number of combinations, at least theoretically, will be the limit imposed by the formulas for all possible permutations and combinations. Strictly speaking, then, such a thing as Jamesian style does not exist in the text. It is an abstraction containing a long list of features which do not all occur together, except for great stretches of discourse beyond the grasp of our immediate perception—whole novels or entire periods in an author's life. We recognize any given passage as Jamesian only by degree, the degree to which the passage contains a number of the features from our individual lists, and the lists differ from reader to reader. This is why no statistical count can document the "subjective impressions" of a reader. Statistics cannot account for our "impression" of what makes a feature significant in the first place.

Both Bennison Gray and Gary Sloan have argued that abstract features of diction and syntax have little or nothing to do with our ability to associate certain individual passages of prose with their supposed authors. Gray asserts that the entire concept of style is metaphoric, that style is simply the sum total of everything an author has written. According to Gray, we only recognize a style through the particulars of what an author is talking about, and therefore, if we are able to identify a passage as being written by a particular author we are only recognizing his subject matter.[8] Sloan supports Gray's hypothesis with a study of ten prose passages of about one thousand words each from Milton to Arnold and Mill. After he altered the passages slightly to "foster a disassociation of subject matter and author and, in some cases, promote new but erroneous associations," Sloan gave the passages to twenty professors from three universities, all of whom were then teaching or had recently taught survey courses in British literature, and asked them to identify the authors. No more than three of the twenty professors correctly identified any one of the unknown authors, and three chose the correct author only once. In four cases, only two of the professors correctly identified the author; in another four cases only one did. Equally remarkable was the range of responses: for any given passage there were nine to fifteen different guesses.[9] Clearly, our ability to abstract purely stylistic features from a text or a variety of texts by a single author is a difficult and very personal matter.

In its extreme form, however, Gray's position is that of the medieval nominalists—only particulars are real; concepts and abstractions are not. Gray's argument cannot account for our ability to recognize parodies, in which certain formal aspects of style remain the same but "content" differs. Without some sense of the formal features of a Jamesian text, for example, how would we be able to recognize this as a parody:

> That it hardly was, that it all bleakly and unbeguilingly *wasn't* for "the likes" of him—poor decent Stamfordham—to rap out queries about the owner of the to him unknown and unsuggestive name that had, in these days, been thrust on him with such a wealth of commendatory gesture, was precisely what now, as he took, with his prepared list of New Year *colifichets* and whatever, his way to the great gaudy palace, fairly flicked his cheek with the sense of his having never before so let himself in, as he ruefully phrased it, without letting anything, by the same token, out.[10]

Indeed, we may not even recognize this as a parody until later in the story. Only if we note the redundancy in the opening two clauses, only if we get a sense that even for James this sentence is rather long and complicated, only if we stop to ponder the fact that the quirks come a little too fast and thick will we recognize that this sentence is not quite what it should be. The devices are clearly ones that James uses; they just do not seem to imply as much as James usually does.

Nevertheless, if I am right, if we only build up a concept of James' style from actually reading James and abstracting certain formal features from the text, then "content," what James is talking about, is unquestionably just as important as how he says it. We form a concept of James' subject matter in the same way that we do so for features of diction and syntax. In *The Wings of the Dove* Kate and Densher at one point see "others" coming out of a "place of purchase," and we immediately recognize that this is the level of abstraction at which James often operates: he does not often name names and call establishments by their trade names.[11] This, of course, accounts for the common description of James' style as abstract or intangible. James' diction is abstract and intangible because he is writing about abstractions and intangible things. *Form* and *content* in this case are identical and interchangeable, and we distinguish between them only to preserve a distinction that can be useful at other times. It is possible, for example, to discuss abstractions in concrete terms and vice versa. The techniques we most often associate with literature—metaphor and symbolism, the concrete universal, the objective correlative—are ways of comprehending and talking about abstractions in specific cases and with concrete examples.

I can dramatize the difference between a personal concept of James' style, a composite of the features we consider significant from a variety of different sources, and the supposed objective data of various statistical studies with a few, albeit simple, statistics of my own. Charles R. Crow in a wonderful essay on *The Wings of the Dove* argues that James' style is not "a slow elaborate monotone" but sufficiently various to accomplish a number of different purposes.[12] Crow has no trouble finding seven sample passages that do not fit the stereotype of James' prose. The passages Crow cites are specific and concrete, they avoid passive verbs, and they lack many of the mannerisms we often associate with James. Here, for example, is a description of Kate Croy from the opening chapter:

1. She stared into the tarnished glass too hard indeed to be staring at her beauty alone. 2. She readjusted the poise of her black, closely-feathered hat; retouched, beneath it, the thick fall of her dusky hair; kept her eyes, aslant, no less on her beautiful averted than on her beautiful presented oval. 3. She was dressed altogether in black, which gave an even tone, by contrast, to her clear face and made her hair more harmoniously dark. 4. Outside, on the balcony, her eyes showed as blue; within, at the mirror, they showed almost as black. 5. She was handsome, but the degree of it was not sustained by items and aids; a circumstance moreover playing its part at almost any time in the impression she produced. 6. The impression was one that remained, but as regards the sources of it no sum in addition would have made up the total. 7. She had stature without height, grace without motion, presence without mass. 8. Slender and simple, frequently soundless, she was somehow always in the line of the eye—she counted singularly for its pleasure. 9. More "dressed," often, with fewer accessories, than other women, or less dressed, should occasion require, with more, she probably could not have given the key to these felicities. 10. They were mysteries of which her friends were conscious—those friends whose general explanation was to say that she was clever, whether or no it were taken by the world as the cause or as the effect of her charm. 11. If she saw more things than her fine face in the dull glass of her father's lodgings, she might have seen that, after all, she was not herself a fact in the collapse. 12. She didn't judge herself cheap, she didn't

make for misery. 13. Personally, at least, she was not chalk-marked for the auction. 14. She hadn't given up yet, and the broken sentence, if she was the last word, *would* end with a sort of meaning. (WOD, I, 5–6)

Seymour Chatman found that a "representative" passage of 200 sentences from *The Wings of the Dove* had the following characteristics, which I have compared with the passage cited by Crow in table 1.

Table 1
Comparison of Passages Cited by Chatman and Crow
(*in percentage*)

Subjects of Main Clauses	Chatman	Crow
Active Agents	55	68.2
Tangible Nouns	1	4.6
Intangible Nouns	44	27.3
Deictic Pronouns	15	9.1
Expletives	89	0

Chatman found his passage overwhelmingly dominated by verbs of mental action; yet in the description of Kate Croy, I find only two: "She might have seen that, after all, she was not herself a fact in the collapse" and "she didn't judge herself cheap." We may consider three other verbs as referring to mental activity if we take them as statements of Kate exercising her will to achieve certain ends: "she didn't make for misery," "she hadn't given up yet," "and the broken sentence . . . would end with a sort of meaning." The reason for the disparity in the kinds of verbs James uses is obvious. In Chatman's passage a character is thinking; Crow's passage is primarily a description.

If we run through the list of thirteen features which various critics have asserted are characteristic—or at least noteworthy—about Jamesian style, we will see the same sort of disparity continually. I find no active agents in oblique grammatical positions because they have been displaced by intangible nouns, although Kate does appear as the subject in two subordinate clauses (in sentences 5 and 14). Only one sentence uses the past perfect tense (sentence 14). Only one sentence uses what R. W. Short calls a "loose" conjunction (once again, sentence 14). Only one sentence uses a semicolon with a participial construction (sentence 5). True, the passage does contain as many as five of the famous parenthetical interruptions, but none of them is very odd, with the possible exception of sentence 9: "More 'dressed,' often, with fewer

accessories, than other women, or less dressed, should occasion require, with more." (See also sentences 2, 11, and 14.) There are two
conditionals, but both are clearly hypothetical and not ambiguous
(sentences 11 and 14). I detect only one logical term (sentence 6: "no
sum in addition would have made up the total") and only two colloquial
two-word verbs, only one of which is odd ("she didn't make for misery"
in sentence 12; the other is "she hadn't given up" in sentence 14).
Likewise, there is only one italicized word (*would* in sentence 14). I
find none of these characteristics so prominent that I would immediately assert that this passage was written by Henry James if I ran
across it listed anonymously in an anthology. In fact, it seems to me
that only sentences 9 and 14 give even the slightest hint of the kind
of prose we usually associate with James. Chatman would reply, of
course, that this passage, which is only about three hundred words
long, is a highly selective sample and hardly typical. But that is just
my point. Most passages of close reading by impressionist critics approximate three hundred words or less.[13] About three hundred words
seems to be the upper limit of our ability to perceive and argue the
significance of a set of features in context. In addition, we do not come
by our individual concepts of James' style by noting random samples.
We build up our concept of James' style most often by noting what
seems significant at crucial moments in the story, when certain elements are important for a complex of reasons having to do with our
perception of the entire point and movement of the story as a whole,
when we pay attention to the language itself because at those times
the language seems—for purely personal reasons—more important
than at other times.

What is significant about the description of Kate Croy are precisely
those features which Chatman finds most untypical of James: the short
sentences, the repeated *"she* + predicate" which, to Crow, project
Kate's "hard vitality." To Crow, this passage represents James at his
best; it represents what we read James for, and to argue that somehow
it is not typical is decidedly to miss the point. Our concept of James'
style must include this and other passages, typical or not, the entire
range of what an author is capable, "the means by which come those
insights we now value in James."[14]

I do not mean to suggest that all of our personal impressions of style
must come from key moments or be related to thematic concerns. A
characteristic I often associate with James' late style is his "preference
for *p*'s." At certain moments James breaks out into alliteration. Here,
for example, are all the instances of alliteration in the first two para-

graphs of section 9 of "The Beast in the Jungle": "superlative sanctity," "vulgar and vain," "for proof or pride," "settled to his safety," "met him before in mildness—not, as before, in mockery," "to confess of themselves to the connection," "as a positive resource; he carried out his periodical returns," "not wandering she, but stationary still." (BIJ, 396–98) I have no idea how often James uses such alliteration, and for the life of me I cannot think of any reason why he should. Regarding this feature of Jamesian prose, I have neither the precise evidence of Chatman nor the aesthetic rationale of Crow. I have simply noted the alliteration, and when I think of James' prose I often think of alliteration. No amount of statistical evidence to the contrary and no lack of an aesthetic justification is going to make me not think of alliteration as an aspect of James' style. A similar feature which confounds critics is James' use of logical terms. I have seen no evidence for how often they occur, and I have read no convincing rationale for why James uses them. They are simply what I have noted, as have Dorothea Krook and Vernon Lee as well as Seymour Chatman.[15]

In a sense, then, James' style is what we make of it, what we notice for reasons of our own, what we use to document our critical judgments. James' style is a function of our own interests and our own critical procedures. When we characterize James' style as complex or ponderous and satisfying, when we claim that it is revealing or profound or well suited to James' purposes, we are making an assertion based on a kind of perception and a kind of judgment that goes far beyond word counts, percentages, and frequencies of distribution. So when we read stylistic analyses, we must pay as much attention to the ultimate claims of the critic and the procedures he uses as to his characterization of the prose. Such claims and procedures are intimately bound up with what the critic perceives in the text and may even determine what he noticed in the first place. It is perhaps because they sense the limitations of their methods that most scholars who use the statistical-comparative method continually make judgments and interpretations that transcend their data. Mere facts do not seem to be enough; we want to know what the facts are for, what these scholars make of them. At times, however, because they are so concerned with facts and figures and not with the nature of critical judgments, scholars who do use the statistical-comparative method can make critical judgments that are very questionable. Thus Leo Hendrick can claim than a complicated subject matter results in a complicated style and William Smith that a unique style (by which Smith means one dominated by simple sentences) is justified by a unique subject matter (an interest in things in and of themselves).[16] Two more sophisticated claims of the same kind are these:

> A periodic sentence offers, in this sense, a way of escaping from the "tyranny of succession," for although meanings are necessarily presented sequentially, periodic structure requires us to hold them all in the mind simultaneously. Thus, an apparently needless complication of style, such as James' predilection for parenthetical constructions, may find its justification in the impression that it gives of complex wholeness.[17]

> Of course, our chief interest in the penchant for ellipsis in James' style is esthetic; that is, we wonder about its functions in the total effect of his fiction. One of these surely is the 'screening' among readers. . . . Another, I think, is the heavy sense of *portent* noted by Watt and other critics.[18]

Judgments such as these are not verifiable by statistics or comparisons. The first asserts that style is expressive, and the second that style can imitate or reproduce its subject matter. I deal with the first in chapter 4 and the second in chapter 5.

4. *Style as Expression*

If, then, we are free to make of James' late style what we can, what do we make of it? What are we to say about such Jamesian sentences as this one from *The Golden Bowl?*

> It may be mentioned also that he [Adam Verver] always figured other persons—such was the law of his nature—as a numerous array, and that, though conscious of but a single near tie, one affection, one duty deepest-rooted in his life, it had never, for many minutes together, been his portion not to feel himself surrounded and committed, never quite been his refreshment to make out where the many-coloured human appeal, represented by gradations of tint, diminishing concentric zones of intensity, of importunity, really faded to the blessed impersonal whiteness for which his vision sometimes ached. (GB, I, 126)

Like William James, I find myself woefully at a loss to say anything significant about this kind of sentence at all, except to express my dismay. I read it again and again. I note the features of James' style that I pointed out earlier: the intangible nouns to describe Verver's situation and desire (people as an "array," Maggie as "a single near tie," Verver's relationship to people other than Maggie as an "appeal" with "diminishing concentric zones of intensity"), the parenthetical interruptions ("such was the law of his nature," "for many minutes together"), the elaborate metaphor of Verver's acquaintances as a "many-coloured human appeal" graduated in tint in contrast to his desire for impersonal whiteness, the double negative ("it had never . . . been his portion not to feel"). I try to apply traditional rhetorical concepts such as tone and looseness or periodicity. I note the slight authorial intrusion of "it may also be mentioned that," which reminds me of the omniscient narrator, always in control. I note the clinical detachment of the narrator as he analyzes Verver's inner mental state. I note that the sentence really is periodic and builds to a kind of climax, the object of Verver's desire, the blessed whiteness of impersonality, after the long elaboration of what prevents him from achieving his goal. I try to understand the sentence in context. It comes near the end of the opening paragraph of the seventh chapter, the beginning of book 2, and it is part of our first introduction to Adam Verver himself, as opposed to what others think of him. This opening description seems to confirm the mystery that the Prince found in Verver in the first book. I, too, do not know what to make of a man who desires so much to retreat from the world and still manipulate it to his advantage.

I can go on characterizing the sentence like this, describing it in various terms and using various categories, but I feel that my description somehow misses the point. With its abstract diction and interrupted syntax, its almost willful flouting of the usual standards for clear prose, the sentence does indeed seem to border, if not on nonsense, then at least on a level of abstraction very difficult for a normal reader of fiction to comprehend for an extended period of time. If we have to stop and parse out the meaning of a novel sentence by sentence and phrase by phrase, we may lose any sense of the story as a whole and wonder whether the effort is worth it. Once again, I need to remind myself of Marvin Bell's words: "The natural end and extension / of language / is nonsense. Yet there is safety / only there."

One way critics have come to grips with James' late style is by asserting that, if nothing else, the style is expressive: it embodies or projects certain aesthetic qualities, or it implies something about the author, either James himself or an "implied author." The notion that language can be expressive is certainly one way of coping with James' style, but the theory of expressive language—and the language we use to talk about expression—explores the limits of language and borders on nonsense just as James' prose does. Let me explain why.

Here are a number of qualities which various critics have found in James' late prose:

"Its features include poise and rotundity, amplitude and opulence, eloquence and poetry." (Darshan Singh Maini)[1]

"The texture of euphuistic prose, woven of *figurae verborum,* as opposed to *figurae sententiae,* produces a diffuse or floating effect." (R.W. Short)[2]

James' syntactic interruptions and qualifications "lend his prose an air of immediacy." (Jane P. Tompkins)[3]

Ellipsis in "The Beast in the Jungle" and other later works produces "a heavy sense of portent." (Seymour Chatman)[4]

"Thus an apparently needless complication of style, such as James' predilection for parenthetical constructions, may find its justification in the impression it gives of complex wholeness." (Geoffrey Leech and Michael Short)[5]

"Poise and rotundity, amplitude and opulence, eloquence and poetry," "a diffuse or floating effect," "an air of immediacy," "a heavy sense of portent," and "the impression of complex wholeness"—all of these qualities are expressed by James' prose, or at least such qualities have been perceived by various critics at various times in response to their reading different passages of James' work. I think we all recognize that such judgments are subjective and personal, but how much validity do they have? That is, how well-grounded or justified are these judgments? If they are based on a system of inference, how correctly are they derived from their premises? Or more broadly, on what basis are they made in the first place?

Perhaps we can confront these theoretical issues more specifically if we apply the critical responses to James' late style to the passage I have already quoted from *The Golden Bowl.* In that sentence I do not feel "an air of immediacy" created by the interruptions and qualifications; in fact, I feel just the opposite, a sense of prolongation and perhaps even needless complication. But Tompkins is describing passages from "The Beast in the Jungle" and it is possible that the same grammatical form can produce different qualities in different contexts. I detect nothing of what Chatman calls "ellipsis" in the passage, so his judgment does not apply. Neither, however, do I find this sentence poised or rotund, eloquent or poetic—ample and opulent, perhaps; eloquent and poetic, no. Indeed, I find it closer to what F. R. Leavis calls "coloured diagram." I think I do understand Short's notion that James' metaphors produce "a floating effect," a sense on first reading that I am skimming along on the surface of great depths, but when I have to stop and puzzle out the meaning, as I had to do with this sentence, the floating effect quickly disappears. As for Leech and Short's notion that the parentheses suggest "complex wholeness" I do not know. I am not sure if the sentence here is complex or merely dense and abstract. True, after I have pondered the point, I sense that Verver has been carefully, even minutely, characterized, but I think the phrase "complex wholeness" is excessive. I know one aspect of Verver's character now and that one aspect has been stated with some complexity, but whether the syntax conveys "wholeness" is another matter. I am not sure what the word means in this situation.

So in some cases I agree with the judgments of others that James' style expresses certain qualities, in some other cases, I disagree, and in still other cases I am not even certain what the assertions mean. What is going on here? What is going on, it seems to me, is that we are all applying our own private perceptions and tastes and plugging our discriminations and evaluations into the only words available, those public words which must express each of our private experiences—a perfectly impossible task. We are noting certain features of James' prose, we are associating those features with certain qualities, either immediately or after some study, and we are proclaiming that the qualities we have noted are somehow "in" the prose as a kind of convention, because we have no other way to talk about such qualities. It would be equally misleading to proclaim that the qualities we discovered in James' style were "in" us. Above all, I think we must affirm that the process of arriving at judgments of expressiveness in style is entirely a matter of personal discrimination and association; judgments of expressiveness do not involve a process of induction or inference. We have no standards for expressiveness to apply to literature or "realize" while reading. There is no necessary correlation between any given feature of a text and what it expresses, what aestheticians call "necessary and sufficient conditions" for a feature to imply a certain quality. I may find that the sentence describing Adam Verver expresses amplitude and opulence because of certain features it contains—because of the length of the extended metaphor or because of the number of abstract nouns ("appeal," "gradations," "zones of intensity," "importunity," "whiteness of vision"), but these features do not intrinsically convey amplitude or opulence, and in another context they most probably would not. Neither do amplitude and opulence have to be expressed by extended metaphors and abstract diction. They may be expressed in other ways—by parallelism, for example, or by very concrete descriptions of miscellaneous details.

We do not, then, read about Adam Verver, note the number of abstract nouns and the extended metaphor, and conclude by induction that so many abstractions thereby must make the passage ample and opulent. Neither do we recognize that the abstract nouns and the extended metaphor meet a certain standard of amplitude and opulence and thereby infer that the passage is ample and opulent because it contains those features. Rather, we recognize expressiveness by what Alan Tormey calls "the fusion of perception and choice."[6] We note certain features, we associate those features with certain other characteristics or effects, and we label those characteristics or effects as best we can. We do not reason as such at all.

Frank Sibley distinguishes between aesthetic and nonaesthetic terms. By aesthetic terms Sibley means terms such as these: *unified, balanced, integrated, lifeless, serene, somber, dynamic, powerful, vivid, delicate, moving, trite, sentimental, tragic.* And by nonaesthetic terms he means the following:

> We say that a novel has a great number of characters and deals with life in a manufacturing town; that a painting uses pale colors, predominantly blues and greens, and has kneeling figures in the foreground; that the theme of a fugue is inverted at such a point and that there is a stretto at the close; that the action of a play takes place in the span of one day and that there is a reconciliation scene in the fifth act. Such remarks may be made by, and such features pointed out to, anyone with normal eyes, ears, and intelligence.[7]

In short, according to Sibley, such remarks do not involve taste or perceptiveness or sensitivity, the hallmarks of aesthetic judgment.

Sibley's point in making the distinction between aesthetic and nonaesthetic terms is that we cannot cite nonaesthetic terms in such a way that "the presence of some set or number of them will beyond question logically justify or warrant the application of an aesthetic term."[8] Or to put it another way: "there are no nonaesthetic features which serve in *any* circumstances as logically *sufficient conditions* for applying aesthetic terms. Aesthetic or taste concepts are not in *this* respect conditioned-governed at all."[9] Sibley goes on to argue that the nonaesthetic characteristics of an artwork may limit the range of the aesthetic terms we could apply ("taste concepts may be governed negatively"): we would not ordinarily call a story tragic if the hero and heroine live happily ever after. But there are no features of a text that would necessarily establish it as tragic. The depiction of death and suffering may be a feature of texts which leads us toward applying the term *tragic,* but no amount of death and suffering can necessarily establish a novel or story as tragic. Murder mysteries—those of Raymond Chandler, for example—contain a great deal of death and suffering, but we do not think of them as tragic.

Nevertheless, even though we use what Sibley calls aesthetic terms—and what I am calling assertions of expressiveness—without rules or conditions, we can defend our judgments and try to convince others of their appropriateness. Sibley lists seven ways we can do so, the most important being simply to point out the nonaesthetic features of an artwork and call for agreement.

Although I find Sibley's argument persuasive, and the best statement of my own views, there are any number of difficulties with it. The major difficulty is pointed out by W. E. Kennick in his anthology of essays on aesthetics:

> Sibley holds that *no* description of a work of art in nonaesthetic terms, "however full," warrants our saying that it is coherent or powerful; "even with the help of precise names, or even samples and illustrations, of particular shades of color, contours, and lines, any attempt to state conditions would be futile." On the other hand, he holds that "on *seeing* the picture we might say, and rightly, that it is coherent or powerful." Now what does seeing a picture give the viewer that no description, however full, *can* give, as far as the correct application of aesthetic terms is concerned? If what we see in the picture are the features that "make" it coherent or powerful, why *can't* a description of these features warrant our saying that it is? Can't anything that is visible be described? If not, what is the obstacle? If it can, then we can describe what makes a picture coherent, and what is that but a sufficient condition?[10]

The answer to Kennick, it seems to me, is clear from the point of view I have been putting forward all along. No description of an artwork can be completely full. What I read in a story is not necessarily what someone else reads in a story, and when I isolate certain features as examples of what caused me to make my judgment, I destroy the context that produced the judgment. Only those particular features in that particular context made those features coherent and powerful. Aesthetic judgment can only be exercised about particulars. All forms of argument about expression are variations of this argument: "See! See! See not just that but that! Not just that but that! Isn't that coherent and powerful?" It is not the features themselves but the features in context that are coherent and powerful, and only a reproduction of my experience of that context can produce the same judgment.

I can whole-heartedly agree with certain judgments about the expressiveness of James' late style for the very reasons pointed out by Sibley. The critics making these judgments have indicated, as much as is humanly possible, those features in James' style that caused them to think of that style as ample and opulent, floating or immediate. And often when I do not understand an expressive term, such as "complex wholeness," it is because the critic in question has not provided me with sufficient examples. In some cases, however, no amount of evidence will make me agree with a judgment of expressiveness because I do not associate the features in question with the same aesthetic qualities. It is only in rare cases, for example, that I find James' late style "immediate" or "eloquent" or "poetic." It seems to me that we cannot really justify James' late style by saying it is expressive, unless we deal with what Sibley has called the "negative conditions" which limit our application of certain terms. A great deal of my ability to appreciate James' prose as "immediate" or "eloquent" or "poetic" is limited by my recognition of other qualities that I can only label as clumsy, awkward, dense, obscure, forbidding, even pointless. If these qualities are not immediately recognizable in the passage I have already cited from *The Golden Bowl,* here is another from *The Wings of the Dove:* "she required much reminding before it came back to her that she had mentioned to this companion just afterwards the confidence expressed by the personage in question in her never doing so dire a thing as to come to London without, as the phrase was, looking a fellow up." (WOD, I, 136) Ian Watt has called James' use of synonyms and pronouns "elegant variation," but I doubt if even Watt would want to label as eloquent "this companion" and "the personage in question," to say nothing of the needless complexity of, by my count, five clauses embedded in each other. Any critic who wants to defend James' style as eloquent or poetic must, it seems to me, confront such "negative conditions."

One final comment about arguments that James' style expresses certain aesthetic qualities: expressiveness is not usually an end in itself. We do not read James merely to experience "a floating effect" or "an impression of immediacy." Usually, such effects or impressions accompany and complement our perception of a larger purpose in the work we are reading, and thus it seems to me that no style can be adequately explained or justified primarily by the argument that it expresses an aesthetic quality. After all, words "mean" as well as they "imply" or "express," and we read James primarily for what he says. Any defense of James' late style must confront the larger issue of what the expressiveness of his language helps to convey.

But critics of Jamesian style also argue that language can be expressive of other things besides aesthetic qualities: language can, for example, express something about the mind or personality of the author. This argument comes in two forms: the "strong" argument that James' style indicates something of his actual personality or state of mind, and the "weak" argument that James' style is a projection of a certain *persona,* a recognizable personality which we cannot associate with James himself but which we can associate with a nameless narrator who gives the writing a certain character.

A good example of the "strong" argument is given by Richard Ohmann, who asserts that authorial "intuition" is analogous to linguistic competence and therefore "a stylistic intuition proceeds from, and evokes, a way of experiencing, and literary styles are closely allied to styles of perception and styles of cognition."[11] Ohmann analyzes one of James' sentences from *The American Scene,* notes the deletion of a great number of "human agents or observers or receivers of impressions" from a hypothetical deep structure, and concludes that these "suppressed relations" are the reason "for our awareness that we are in the presence of a mind playing over experience in an exceedingly fastidious way."[12] Ohmann does not claim that James went about consciously deleting human nouns from his writing, but he does claim that the deletion of human agents is an indication of the fundamental way James perceived reality:

> And in general, I think that when a critic describes and analyzes a style, he is trying to describe that intuition [of the writer], trying to make explicit the constraints that the writer imposes on himself, in large part unconsciously, in order to present his vision of things. If so, the critic is to that extent a crypto-psycho-linguist, or possibly a psycho-crypto-linguist.[13]

There are, it seems to me, two criteria for the critic to meet, if he wants to become a crypto-psycho-linguist. First, he must provide evidence from outside the text that the author in question did in fact have the personality trait manifested in the style. As it stands, Ohmann's argument is no different from the argument that style can express an aesthetic quality. His only evidence that James was in fact fastidious is the passage from *The American Scene.* Ohmann ignores the possibility that a passage of prose may express qualities contrary to the personality of the author. There is, after all, no necessary reason why a crude, vulgar person in everyday life cannot write fastidious prose. The history of literature is full of novelists and poets who were delicate craftsmen in their writing but whose personal lives were often rough and rude. Dylan Thomas is just one recent example. Thus the crypto-psycho-linguist must establish the characteristics of an author's style and the traits of his personality independently, if he wants to assert that one reflects the other. Second, the critic must provide evidence that those features of an author's style which reflect his personality are not limited to a single genre but express his personality across a range of discourse. Otherwise, we have no way of knowing whether the writer merely adopted a particular personality trait or *persona* for the sake of a single work or a particular genre. If a stylistic feature is limited to a particular kind of rhetorical situation or a particular form of discourse, we have good reason for thinking that the feature does not reflect a fundamental method of perceiving or conceiving reality but merely the exigencies of the moment. Ohmann presents no evidence that James' deletion of human agents occurs in a variety of discourse.

Despite the lack of a necessary correlation between the style and the man, critics have persisted in seeing the late style as evidence for James' psychological state at the end of his life. Darshan Singh Maini presents a number of these speculations: he states that the late style could have resulted from James' method of dictating to a typist after about 1897, from a shift in vision, an imagination "increasingly straining at the leash," or from various psychological pressures, such as James' "hyper-sensitive awareness and regard for the swarm of doubts and shy contingencies that clamoured for utterance at every turn of one's thought," or his concern for "personal privacies," his caution and prevarication, or even his sexuality, either his "sexually starved life" or the opposite, "the eruption of delayed sexuality."[14] All of this is speculation. Maini offers no evidence other than a few brief quotations from James' fiction that any of these claims is true.

There are, as far as I know, only two studies that deal seriously and systematically with the issue of what the late style may tell us about James' personality. The first is by John Halverson in an article entitled "Late Manner, Major Phase" for the *Sewanee Review*. In that article Halverson argues that the abstract diction and syntactic complexity of the late style were necessary in order for James to confront the problem of evil. According to Halverson, during James' middle period "his craft developed," but "his moral conceptions remained static." Both *The*

Bostonians at the beginning of the period and *What Maisie Knew* at the end contain "cardboard figures of malevolence." Beginning with "The Turn of the Screw," however, James began to look at evil "from the inside," and thus he "reveals—and perhaps himself comes to see— that evil is itself no simple black-and-white matter; it too is terribly ambiguous."[15] And the price James paid for this "psychological and moral penetration," according to Halverson, is that "he loses sight altogether of the verbal splendors of his earlier style":

> Most of the peculiarities of the late manner are traceable to this preoccupation. The extraordinarily abstract diction, for example, is a product of the long and often painful attempt to grasp essences, somehow to get at the real thing. . . . He is not so much narrating a concrete story which would serve iconically to represent the intellectual generalities, as he is working out the generalities in the narration. Not inevitably, but at least understandably, his diction becomes highly abstract. . . .
>
> The attempt to understand as completely as possible leads also to syntactical complexity. No observation can be both simple and true; it must be qualified and qualified. . . . Before the mystery of goodness James stands awe-stricken and linguistically desperate, as if overwhelmed by his own discovery. Indeed, awe infuses the whole range of psychological and moral discovery as James finds and reveals layer after layer of complexity in the tortuous process of understanding.[16]

The primary evidence Halverson offers for this extraordinary argument is from the late novels: he cites their moral complexity and offers a number of examples of their "indiscriminate" syntactic complexity. He presents no evidence from outside the novels—from letters or journals, from biographical sources—that James was preoccupied with the nature of evil more at the end of his career than he had been throughout his entire life. Halverson does, however, try to demonstrate that the late style had become a mere habit with James. He notes the way all of the characters in the late novels sound alike and how they all sound like James, he cites A. C. Benson on James' oral monologues, how James could construct "a little palace of thought of improvised yet perfect design," to show the similarity between his oral and written styles, and he repeats the famous anecdote by Edith Wharton, who asked James why he had left the four main characters of *The Golden Bowl* in such a void. James replied: "My dear—I didn't know I had."[17]

Halverson's argument hinges on the assertion that the late novels are morally complex in spite of the style, that the style is the result of a mere habit which allowed James the freedom to think about more serious matters. In making this assertion, Halverson is depriving James of one of the major characteristics which we associate with great writers: his control over his material. There is, I think, something to Halverson's argument, but he puts it in an extreme form. A great many of the mannerisms we associate with James—beginning a sentence with a pronoun, the referent following in parentheses; the parenthetical interruptions at odd places, the oddly italicized words, all of those devices for which we can discover no adequate aesthetic rationale— may be "mere habit," but to argue that most of the late style was not a result of James' artistic choice flies in the face of James' many defenses of his style, especially to brother William but also to others, and the fact that his writing late in his life was sufficiently various to make the late style clearly one way of writing among others—something I plan to demonstrate in a moment. Whether the late style had to become a habit in order for James to more seriously confront the nature of evil is, it seems to me, an interesting speculation for which there can be no adequate evidence one way or the other.

The other critic who deals with the connection between James' late style and his personality is Richard Hocks, who argues in his book *Henry James and Pragmatistic Thought* that "William James' prag- matistic thought is literally *actualized* as the literary art and idiom of his brother Henry James, especially so in the later work."[18] Hocks reviews William's argument for "ambulatory" relations in *The Meaning of Truth* (1909) as the key to William's notion of cognition as "made out of intervening parts of experience through which we ambulate in succession." Hocks comments:

> What he [William] has done above all is to make knowing
> continually dramatic, a "happening" if you will. Similarly to
> *Pragmatism* where truth is "itself an event," he now conceives the
> knowing process as a continual event, for intervening
> experiences, like "intervening space" in distance relationships,
> must be mentally grasped as real "territory" and thus made living
> and present, the sacredness of each "intermediary" as important
> as Henry's nuances and "shades" of meaning.[19]

Thus, for Hocks, Henry's late style is an embodiment of the open- ended way Henry "characteristically sees an issue," or an even bolder assertion, Henry's "language—his choice of words, his syntax, even his punctuation—may be useful in determining not just what he 'thinks' about a matter, but how he is think*ing.*"[20] The primary evidence Hocks uses to illustrate the connections between James' language and his mode of thought is a letter James wrote to Henry Adams in March of 1914. Adams' letter has not survived, but apparently Adams had expressed some pessimism about the events of 1914 and questioned the efficacy of art, perhaps including James' latest volume, *Notes of a Son and a Brother.* James' letter is as follows:

My Dear Henry [Adams], I have your melancholy outpouring of the 7th, and I know not how better to acknowledge it than by the full recognition of its unmitigated blackness. *Of course* we are lone survivors, of course the past that was our lives is at the bottom of an abyss—if the abyss *has* any bottom; of course, too, there's no use talking unless one particularly *wants* to. But the purpose, almost, of my printed divagations was to show you that one *can,* strange to say, still want to—or at least can behave as if one did. Behold me therefore so behaving—and apparently capable of continuing to do so. I still find my consciousness interesting—under *cultivation* of the interest. Cultivate it *with* me, dear Henry—that's what I hoped to make you do—to cultivate yours for all that it has in common with mine. *Why* mine yields an interest I don't know that I can tell you, but I don't challenge or quarrel with it—I encourage it with a ghastly grin. You see I still, in the presence of life (or of what you deny to be such,) have reactions—as many as possible—and the book I sent you is a proof of them. It's, I suppose, because I am that queer monster, the artist, an obstinate finality, an inexhaustible sensibility. Hence the reactions—appearances, memories, many things, go on playing upon it with consequences that I note and "enjoy" (grim word!) noting. It all takes doing—and I *do.* I believe I shall do yet again—it is still—an act of life. But you perform them still yourself—and I don't know what keeps me from calling your letter a charming one! There we are, and it's a blessing that you understand—I admit indeed alone—your all-faithful [Signed] Henry James.[21]

Hocks finds this letter a perfect example of Henry's characteristic mode of thought: the letter illustrates "a mind thoroughly at odds with fixed values or meanings" and open to all experience because James "acknowledges" and "recognizes" Adams' "unmitigated blackness" without passing *a priori* judgment on it; the letter shows James cutting the fundamental questions of Adams' despair and the efficacy of art down to what he can know, what he knows about the questions empirically: in this case, the urge to talk about these questions; the letter exhibits the irony, the cordiality, and the acceptance of Henry's "felt life" or William's "felt experience," the ability to elaborate on a "germ" in order to celebrate consciousness, unifying experience into "a dramatic and continuing experience," primarily through the use of subordinate clauses and parentheses; in this case the elaboration is on Henry's idea of art and the artist. Openness to experience, the lack of fixed values or meanings, the incorporation of opposites, irony, cordiality and acceptance, an emphasis on the actual and the concrete—these are the characteristics which Hocks finds embodied in the late style and which he thinks express the essence of James' method of perceiving and thinking about experience.

I find Hocks' argument very persuasive, primarily because it meets the first criterion I established for arguments of this kind: Hocks cites evidence other than the fiction that James indeed had the personality traits he finds exhibited in the late style. Clearly the letter to Adams shows James trying very hard not to contradict Adams and even incorporate Adams's views into his own ("Of course . . . of course . . . of course"). Clearly also the letter shows James elaborating on a "germ" in a display of his consciousness at work, although I do not find the elaboration as "actual" or "empirical" as Hocks does. Hocks also quotes a great deal from the rest of James' writing to show how open and accepting he was, how careful he was to avoid direct confrontations, how unconcerned with philosophical abstractions. What disturbs me about Hocks' argument is the rather casual assertion that all of this is reflected in the late style, especially in the syntax. Of course, Hocks uses the word "style" to refer to the totality of how James wrote, while I have restricted myself to certain elements in that totality, the diction and syntax. Hocks does not deal with James' diction, but he is adamant that James' use of subordinate clauses and parenthetical interruptions captures James' characteristic mode of thought, especially in conjunction with a central intelligence "conjoining and interpenetrating, as one continuous procedure, perceptual materials that otherwise would have to occur in more disjunctive sequence—thus violating to that extent the sort of seamlessness that in real life we often experience between perceiving and thinking."[22] Rather ironically, the letter to Adams which Hocks relies on so heavily is a good example of the dangers in generalizing about an author's style. In many ways, the letter does not fit the hypothetical model of James' style I established earlier. The letter is overwhelmingly dominated by active agents as subjects ("I," "we," "you"), and the sentences are relatively short. True, the letter contains a large number of italicized words and parenthetical interruptions, but the parenthetical interruptions are very often short appositives and about half the dashes introduce not a qualification but an independent clause that sums up or dramatizes the point with a key image. In short, many of the parenthetical interruptions are used not for qualifications but for dramatic effect.

If we want to assert that James' late prose reveals some aspect of his personality, I think that we are going to have to be more precise about what aspects of his prose we are referring to and what aspects of his personality we are talking about. And the way to do so, it seems to me, is to look at a range of discourse written at approximately the same time in order to test whether certain features of the prose cannot be attributed to the demands of a particular genre or at least the writer's conception of that genre, rather than the author's general state of mind or "characteristic mode of thought." If we can also document the writer's mental state at that time from other biographical sources, we may be able to establish more definitely whether there is a connection between the forms of writing and modes of thought. Fortunately, James was a prolific writer, not only of fiction and criticism but also of letters, personal essays, and travelogues. In addition, he kept a journal. By correlating the times that James wrote various letters and journal entries with Leon Edel's report of James' correspondence with James B. Pinker, his agent, I have managed to assemble a representative sample of James' writing in various genres over a period of several months during the winter of 1899 to 1900, just before he began to write *The Sacred Fount*. These writings are listed in figure 5. According to Leon Edel, during the late autumn of 1899 James was "vaguely depressed." He was back from a trip to Italy, which he had found "haunted" because of the popular success of other writers he had known for some time. He was writing letters of "physical, tactile language" to the young sculptor Hendrik Andersen, and was perhaps suffering from a repressed passion for the young man. The house he had lived in for years was up for sale, and James, always insecure about money matters, was trying with considerable anxiety to buy it himself. In addition, while Henry was writing a number of the pieces I have listed, brother William was visiting, still recuperating from a form of heart disease, which had driven him to Bad Nauheim in Germany for a rest before visiting his

Unpublished Writing

Letters

On October 13 to Mrs. A. F. de Navarro and to Sidney Colvin
On November 12 to Edmund Gosse and to Mrs. Henrietta Reubell
On November 20 to H.G. Wells
On November 24 to Charles Eliot Norton

Journal Entries

October 5 and November 11 and 12

Published Writing

Fiction

"The Faces" (later called "The Two Faces"), sent to Pinker on October 11
at a time when James was writing approximately a story a week.

Nonfiction

"The Saint's Afternoon," a travel piece, and "The Future of the Novel," a
piece of criticism for a "universal anthology," both written sometime
in the winter of 1899/1900.

Fig. 5.   Selected writings by James: Winter, 1899/1900.

brother. According to Edel, William's illness was "another—a very loud
clock-stroke of the years."[23] Edel cites many of the themes from the
stories of this period as evidence for James' depression—the revenge
and bad temper and sense of loss in stories such as "The Two Faces,"
"The Special Type," and "The Tone of Time," and the beginning of *The
Sense of the Past,* that extraordinary fragment which is so concerned
with the possibility of a trip into the past and an exchange of person-
alities with the dead. Whether James' depression is manifested in his
style is the question at hand.

If we can rely on the word of Theodora Bosanquet, James' secretary
from 1907 to the end of his life, James' discourse naturally falls into
two categories: journal entries, letters, plays, and the first drafts of
short stories which James wrote out longhand, and full-length novels
and the revisions of the short stories which he dictated to a typist.
James admitted to Bosanquet that dictation caused him to be "too
diffuse."[24] As a result, when a particular project had to be kept strictly
within certain limits, James wrote his drafts out longhand. For short
stories, according to Bosanquet, James "allowed himself a little more
freedom, dictating them from his written draft and expanding them as

he went to an extent which inevitably defeated his original purpose."[25] For novels, James dictated everything from the preliminary character sketches and outline of the plot through all the various revisions to the final form. For the various drafts, "he took pains to pronounce every pronounceable letter, he always spelt out words which the ear might confuse with others, and he never left a single punctuation mark unuttered, except sometimes that necessary point, the full stop."[26] This hardly seems like the behavior of a man for whom dictation had become "mere habit."

The split between James' unpublished writing, which was most often handwritten, and his published work, which was most often dictated, is born out by a comparison of the private and published writing in table 2.

The letters and journal entries contain on average much shorter sentences, many more active agents as subjects, considerably more

Table 2
Features of James' Writing in Various Genres

| Feature | Private | | Published | | |
	Letters	Notebooks	Travel Writing	Criticism	Short Story
Sample Size					
No. of Words	2,651	1,448	3,471	2,329	1,932
No. of Sentences	130	63	93	72	59
Average Sentence Length					
Words/Sentence	20.4	22.98	37.3	32.35	32.75
Percentage of Nominals as Subjects of Main Clauses					
Active Agents	59.2	50.7	19.2	7.2	47.5
Tangible Nouns	5.6	0	14.6	1	5
Intangible Nouns (excluding deictics and expletives)	19	29.6	45	51.5	21.25
Deictic Pronouns	7.8	11.3	8.6	27.8	6.25
Expletives *it/there*	8.4	8.5	12.6	12.4	20
Combined Intangibles	35.2	49.3	66.2	90.7	47.5
Percentage of Verbs in Main Clauses					
Stative	30.1	21.4	50	49	40.7
Active	68.2	78.6	43.6	39.2	54.3
Passive	1.7	0	6.4	11.8	4.9

active verbs, a more direct forceful syntax, and fewer of the mannerisms we associate with James' novels and stories.[27] In some cases, the contrast is especially striking. In the letters, for example, the average sentence length is twelve to fifteen words shorter than in the published fiction and nonfiction (from 20.4 words per sentence in the letters to 37.3 words per sentence in "The Saint's Afternoon"), while active agents as the subject of a sentence occur with much greater frequency (from 59.2 percent of the total in the letters to 7.2 percent in "The Future of the Novel"). Regarding James' use of verbs, I found that, as I suggested earlier, verbs of mental action are entirely dependent on a description of a character thinking so that in a critical essay such as "The Future of the Novel" verbs of mental action virtually disappear. To distinguish among the genres, therefore, I counted stative verbs (forms of *be* and *have* followed by objects or complements), active verbs, and passives in main clauses. Clearly, the letters and journal entries have more active verbs in main clauses by a wide margin (68.2 percent in the letters and 78.6 percent in the journals, as opposed to 43.6 and 39.2 percent in the published nonfiction). (For a more detailed explanation of how I arrived at these figures, see appendix B.)

I have found it impossible to devise a reliable way to measure the relative complexity of James' sentences and the degree to which he interrupts the main flow of his syntax. A tentative count of simple, compound, and complex sentences revealed no great difference among the various genres, and the many ways in which James embeds phrases and clauses within one another defeated my attempt to construct a reliable scale of complexity. Nevertheless, it is clear to me that in the letters and journals James' sentences are less complex than in the published work, if only because they are shorter. A few examples will have to suffice. Here is the opening of James' letter to Henrietta Reubell, in which he discusses his intentions in writing *The Awkward Age:*

Dear Miss Reubell, I have had great pleasure of your last good letter and this is a word of fairly prompt reconnaissance. Your bewilderment over *The Awkward Age* doesn't on the whole surprise me—for that ingenious volume appears to have excited little *but* bewilderment—except indeed, *here,* thick-witted denunciation. A work of art that one has to *explain* fails in so far, I suppose, of its mission. I suppose I must at any rate mention that I had in view a certain special social (highly "modern" and actual) London group and type and tone, which seemed to me to se prêter à merveille to an ironic—lightly and simply ironic!—

treatment, and that clever people at least would know who, in general, and what, one meant. But here, at least, it appears there are very few clever people! One must point with finger-posts—one must label with *pancartes*—one must explain with *conférences*! The *form* doubtless, of my picture is against it—a form all dramatic and scenic—of presented episodes, architecturally combined and each making a piece of the building; with no going behind, *no telling* about the figures save by their own appearance and action and with explanations reduced to the explanation of everything by all the other things *in* the picture. (LET, 333)

Most of the complexity in this letter is entirely a matter of short adjectival or noun clauses ("that one has to explain," "that I had in view a certain special social [highly 'modern' and actual] London group and type and tone"), appositives and prepositional phrases (as in the last sentence). Most of the parenthetical interruptions are short appositives ("lightly and simply ironic!" "a form all dramatic and scenic"). Contrast this kind of complexity with that of longer adverbial clauses, also parenthetically interrupted, in "The Future of the Novel":

But for its subject, magnificently, [the novel] has the whole human consciousness. And if we are pushed to a step farther backward, and asked why the representation should be required when the object represented is itself mostly accessible, the answer to that appears to be that man combines with his eternal desire for more experience an infinite cunning as to getting his experience as cheaply as possible. He will steal it whenever he can. He likes to live the life of others, yet is well aware of the points at which it may too intolerably resemble his own. The vivid fable, more than anything else, gives him knowledge abundant yet vicarious. It enables him to select, to take and to leave; so that to feel he can afford to neglect it he must have a rare faculty, or great opportunities, for the extension of experience—by thought, by emotion, by energy—at first hand. (FN, 33)

The most complex sentence in this passage, the second one, achieves its complexity by a series of embedded clauses: an adverbial clause modifying a noun clause which serves as the object of a verb in another adverbial clause. And in the last sentence an infinitive phrase with a noun clause as its object ("to feel he can afford to neglect it"), which in transformational theory is a deleted form of a longer sentence ("someone feels that"), is embedded in an adverbial clause. When James combined the short appositive interruptions of the letters and the longer, more complex sentences of his published work with a few other mannerisms, such as an inverted sentence order and a preference for deictic pronouns as subjects, he could produce the kind of prose we most often identify as the late style. Here is a selection for James' travel writing, "The Saint's Afternoon," which I hope needs no comment:

> The church-feast of its saint is of course for Anacapri, as for any self-respecting Italian town, the great day of the year, and the smaller the small "country," in native parlance, as well as the simpler, accordingly, the life, the less the chance for leakage, on other pretexts, of the stored wine of loyalty. This pure fluid, it was easy to feel overnight, had not sensibly lowered its level; so that nothing indeed, when the hour came, could well exceed the outpouring. All up and down the Sorrentine promontory the early summer happens to be the time of the saints, and I had just been witness there of a week on every day of which one might have travelled, through kicked-up clouds and other demonstrations, to a different hot holiday. There had been no bland evening that, somewhere or other, in the hills or by the sea, the white dust and the red glow didn't rise to the dim stars. Dust, perspiration, illumination, conversation—these were the regular elements. (SA, 350)

If we compare this passage with the direct simplicity of a more typical letter, one not concerned with the problems of art, we will see the full range of James' style. Here is the beginning of a letter to Sidney Colvin, written in October of 1899, in which James discusses his reaction to a collection of letters by Robert Louis Stevenson:

> My dear Colvin, Many things hindered my quietly and immediately reabsorbing the continuity of the two gathered volumes, and I have delayed till this the acknowledgment of your letter (sent a few days after them,) I having already written (hadn't I?) before the letter arrived. I have spent much of the last two days with them—beautifully and sadly enough. I think you need have no doubt as to the impression the constituted book will make—it will be one of extraordinary rare, particular and individual beauty. I want to write about it really critically, if I can—i.e. intelligently

and interpretatively—but I sigh before the difficulty. Still, I shall probably try. (LET, 330–331)

James' late style is often defended as an oral style because the published work was dictated, and yet, rather ironically, most of the published anecdotes we have that try to capture James' speech show it to be closer to the style of the letters and journals, the handwritten style, than to the style of the published dictated work. The following example from Arthur Benson, who met with James in January of 1900, about the time of the work I have been citing, is typical:

> [James] talked of Mrs. Oliphant, Carlyle—whatever I began.
> "I had not read a line that the poor woman had written for years—not for years; and when she died Henley—do you know him, the rude, boisterous, windy, headstrong Henley?—Henley, as I say, said to me, 'Have you read *Kirsteen?*' I replied that as a matter of fact, no—h'm—I had not read it. Henley said, 'That you should have any pretensions to interest in literature and should dare to say that you have not read *Kirsteen!*' I took my bludgeoning patiently and humbly, my dear Arthur—went back and read it, and was at once confirmed, after twenty pages, in my belief—I laboured through the book—that the poor soul had a simply feminine conception of literature: such slipshod, imperfect, halting, faltering, peeping, down-at-heel work— buffeting along like a ragged creature in a high wind, and just struggling to the goal, and falling in a quivering mass of faintness and fatuity. Yes, no doubt she was a gallant woman— though with no species of wisdom—but an artist, an artist—!" He held up his hands and stared woefully at me.[28]

James' oral style in this and other reconstructions collected in volumes by Simon Nowell-Smith and Norman Page lacks the intangible subjects, the long adverbial clauses, and the complex parenthetical interruptions of the published work.[29] Most of the parenthetical interruptions here are normal occurrences in speech. The only thing unusual is the long list of adjectives to describe Mrs. Oliphant's work, and in this instance James is obviously building up detail for dramatic effect. Page's description of James' speech seems most accurate: "The amplitude of James' slow delivery, his hesitations and repetitions, his groping for the unpredictable but satisfyingly apt word, his rejection of inferior locutions."[30] The complexity of James' speech is one of appositives and lists and parenthetical asides while he was groping for the word he wanted. It is not the complexity of intangibility and subordination. Here is another example from Elisabeth Jordon:

> "Eliminating—ah—(very slow) eliminating—ah—eliminating nine-tenths—(faster) nine-tenths—nine-tenths of—of—of—of (very fast) what he [Henry Savage Landor] claims (slower) of what he claims—of what he claims (very slow) there is still—there is still—there is still (very much faster) enough—left—e-nough left (slower) to make—to—make—to—make—a remarkable record (slow) a remark-able record, (slower) a remarkable record (very slow, with every word heavily emphasised)."[31]

Given the discrepancy between the private and published styles of James' writing, what can we make of the claims that the public late style reflects his preoccupation with evil, his fundamental method of perceiving reality, his vaguely depressed mental state at the time of composition? I think that the validity of such claims is severely diminished. The sheer range of James' diction and syntax precludes any generalizations about his writing as a whole reflecting his mental state or his method of perceiving reality. It is abundantly clear that James could write in a personal active style if he wanted to, but for reasons of his own, in his published work, he chose not to. Brother William constantly nagged at him to write just one novel in an earlier manner simply to prove that he could, and Henry always refused on artistic grounds, as he did in this letter:

> Your reflections on *The Wings of the Dove* greatly interest me. Yet, after all, I don't know that I can very explicitly *meet* them. Or rather, really, there is too much to say. One writes as one *can*— and also as one sees, judges, feels, thinks, and I feel and think so much on the ignoble state to which in this age of every cheapness I see the novel as a form, reduced, that there is doubtless greatly, with me, the element of what I would as well as of what I 'can.' At any rate my stuff, such as it is, is inevitable for me. Of that there is no doubt. But I should think you might well fail of joy in it—for I certainly feel that it is, in its way, more and more positive. Don't despair, however, even yet, for I feel that in its way, as I say, there may be still other variations of way that will more or less *donner le change*.[32]

There remains the argument that James produced the late style not because of a fundamental aspect of his character but because he was seduced by the act of dictation, that his preoccupation with evil or his method of perception only manifested themselves in his published writing. This argument must contend with the fact that in his published writing James does seem to do certain things in similar ways and that these similar techniques transcend the boundaries of genre or subject matter. Are we to assume, then, that James was working out his perception of evil and manifesting his perception of the world just as much in his travelogues and in his literary criticism as in his fiction? It seems to me that we have once again come up against the limits of our ability to say one way or the other. We lack a vocabulary for how perception can be manifested in language. But surely we ought to be able to distinguish between the perception of action and physical reality and the perception of ideas. James, however, makes this distinction very difficult to maintain, indeed. His attempt to describe "impressions" always involves the specification of particulars or the use of metaphor, but his syntax varies considerably and often when he is most engaged in getting at "essences," his syntax is not that complex. We can notice certain common elements in James' public style if we look at three examples of his public writing which deal with his attempt to get at the "essence" of something: to analyze the atmosphere of Italy in his travel writing, the nature of literary appreciation in a piece of criticism, and only in the fiction, to confront the nature of evil. Here is a passage from "The Saint's Afternoon," a travelogue, which analyzes the nature of "beauty" in Italy:

> It threw such difficulties but a step back to say that the secret of the amenity was "style"; for what in the world was the secret of style, which you might have followed up and down the abysmal old Italy for so many a year only to be still vainly calling for it? Everything, at any rate, that happy afternoon, in that place of poetry, was bathed and blessed with it. The castle of Barbarossa had been on the height behind; the villa of black Tiberius had overhung the immensity from the right; the white arcades and the cool chambers offered to every step some sweet old "piece" of the past, some rounded porphyry pillar supporting a bust, some shaft of pale alabaster upholding a trellis, some mutilated marble image, some bronze that had roughly resisted. Our host, if we came to that, had the secret; but he could only express it in grand practical ways. One of them was precisely this wonderful

"afternoon tea," in which tea only—*that*, good as it is, has never the note of style—was not to be found. The beauty and the poetry, at all events, were clear enough, and the extraordinary uplifted distinction. (SA, 354)

In this selection, James is grappling with the nature of "old world style," what he earlier had characterized as the beauty and the horror of Italy. Here he makes the abstraction of beauty more concrete by building up particulars. There is, as far as I can see, only one typical syntactic interruption (in the second to the last sentence), and it is not difficult.

Compare this attempt to get at the nature of beauty with the following passage from "The Future of the Novel," in which James deals with a more abstract essence, that of literary appreciation:

There is to my sense no work of literary, or any other art, that any human being is under the smallest positive obligation to "like." There is no woman—no matter of what loveliness—in the presence of whom it is anything but a man's unchallengeably *own* affair that he is "in love" or out of it. It is not a question of manners; vast is the margin left to individual freedom; and the trap set by the artist occupies no different ground—Robert Louis Stevenson has admirably expressed the analogy—from the offer of her charms by the lady. There only remain infatuations that we envy and emulate. When we do respond to the appeal, when we *are* caught in the trap, we are held and played upon; so that how in the world can there *not* still be a future, however late in the day, for a contrivance possessed of this precious secret? The more we consider it the more we feel the prose picture can never be at the end of its tether until it loses the sense of what it can do. It can do simply everything, and that is its strength and its life. (FN, 35–36)

Here James uses a metaphor to clarify the nature of literary appreciation, to make the essence more concrete: appreciating a novel is like appreciating a woman or being in love. Once again the only typically "Jamesian" sentences are the third and the fifth. The third is a compound with one parenthetical interruption that is not difficult ("Robert Louis Stevenson has admirably expressed the analogy"), and the fifth has a compound introductory adverbial clause and one short parenthetical interruption that does not seem particularly difficult, either ("however late in the day").

Finally, here is a passage from "The Two Faces," a short story, in which James does confront the nature of evil:

What was in the air descended the next moment to earth. He turned round as he caught the expression with which her eyes attached themselves to something that approached. A little person, very young and very much dressed, had come out of the house, and the expression in Mrs. Grantham's eyes was that of the artist confronted with her work and interested, even to impatience, in the judgment of others. The little person drew nearer, and though Sutton's companion, without looking at him now, gave it a name and met it, he had jumped for himself at certitude. He saw many things—too many, and they appeared to be feathers, frills, excrescences of silk and lace—massed together and conflicting, and after a moment also saw struggling out of them a small face that struck him as either scared or sick. Then, with his eyes again returning to Mrs. Grantham, he saw another. (TF, 253)

In this selection, Sutton, the central consciousness of the story, realizes how Mrs. Grantham, angry at being rejected by Lord Gwyther and humiliated by his request that she advise his new wife, had contrived to humiliate in turn the new Lady Gwyther. Mrs. Grantham has allowed the new bride to dress herself in garish fashion at her public debut. Once again, I think this passage is noteworthy for the fact that the style is rather straightforward. "What is in the air" is quickly made more concrete by what Sutton observes in Lady Gwyther's attire, although the specification of "feathers, frills, excrescences of silk and lace" is still somewhat abstract. And once again, except for the long appositive and clause between the dashes in the second to the last sentence, I do not detect any major parenthetical interruptions or many of James' most notorious mannerisms, even though in this selection more than in the other two he is directly confronting what Halverson calls the problem of evil, and even though Edel cites this story as evidence for James' depressed mental state.

There is, then, as far as I can see, little evidence for the "strong" argument that James' style reflects his personality or his state of mind. There is no correlation between any of James' techniques, his use of diction and syntax, and his mental state or his personality, including his preoccupation with evil, except this: James was clearly interested in getting at the essence of things, of wrestling with abstractions, atmosphere, what he called "impressions." But his style is sufficiently various so that I do not think we can claim that certain aspects of his public style resulted from any particular aspect of his personality. Clearly, his diction is abstract when he wants to deal with abstractions, but it is also concrete when he wants to bring his abstractions down to earth. His syntax does not correlate with any particular subject matter or theme.

We are left, then, with the "weak" argument that James' late style projects a persona or an "implied author." Of course, the concept of a persona is clearly hypothetical, a conventional way of talking about the tone or "voice" of a piece of writing, and arguments in favor of a certain persona are also personal and associative, similar to arguments in favor of style as the expression of an aesthetic trait. Thus the problem for the critic is to characterize the persona of the late style and offer an explanation of why James would want to project that kind of personality. As far as I know, no critic has characterized the persona of the late style very thoroughly, but we might variously describe that projected personality as either fastidious or fussy, profound or merely dense and abstract, complex or merely complicated, detailed or preoccupied with minutiae, concerned with nuances or merely with the trivial. The question is why James would wish to project such a controversial persona. Of course, James was trying to appeal to "a discriminating reader" by making fine distinctions, but by using so many features without any apparent larger purpose—the parenthetical interruptions at odd moments, the logical terms, the italicizing of prepositions, the occasional flights of alliteration—he risks projecting a persona which his readers would perceive not as discriminating but as merely mannered, pedantic, and obscure. Given James' desire for a wider reading public, I am hard pressed to provide an aesthetic reason why he would want to sound the way he does.

I can, however, think of a psychological reason why James would want to project such an image. James thought of himself as an artist in a "sacred struggle."[33] In response to brother William's call for greater clarity, he always refers to the "ignoble state" to which the novel has been reduced and argues, although only by implication, that his style is a way of giving his novels greater form, his primary requirement for a great novel. Just how intangible nouns, delayed syntax, and his other mannerisms contribute to the form of his work, James never makes clear, but his commitment to his late style was intimately bound up with his concern for artistic form and his position as an artist. Above all, I think, James wanted to *sound* like an artist. His style was, more than anything else, a result of conscious artistic choice, not for every pause and comma but for a general tone; it was the "voice" with which James wanted to address his public.

There are a number of reasons why James would want to develop the dense magisterial tone of the late style to fulfill his sense of his vocation. For one, he was a shy, sensitive man, a man who in his autobiography constantly compared himself unfavorably with his brother William, a man who was, according to Leon Edel, "too reticent and withdrawn" in his youth to openly woo Minny Temple, a man who fled from the theatre for good after being shouted at and booed during a curtain call, a man who burned most of his papers and asked his friends to burn his letters to them, a man brother William called "very powerless feeling," who needed constant advice and reassurance about how to deal with his servants, buy a house, and meet the other major and minor crises of life.[34] One way for a shy man to assert himself socially, to protect himself from embarrassment and awkwardness is to develop a very formal, very correct manner to provide the proper distance between himself and others. James' elaborate conversational manner, what Norman Page has characterized as "the amplitude of [his] slow delivery," fits this need very well.

But James' speech was not dominated by intangible nouns and complicated subordination, just as his letters and notebooks are not.[35] What drove him to the idiosyncrasies of the late style, I believe, was his concern—we might even call it an obsession—for artistic form and his "sacred" task. When he was composing his public work, James used what I can only call an "aesthetic register." We all know of ministers who have normal conversational manners, but when they are asked to function in their professional roles—to conduct a service, give a sermon, offer a prayer— they shift registers: their voices get louder, their diction becomes more formal, their syntax more elaborate, often in the cadences of the King James version of the Bible. So it was, I believe, with James. Facing the window of his study with his typist behind him waiting for just the right words, the considered judgment of the artist, James slipped into an "aesthetic register" and exaggerated his already formal conversational manner: his interest in essences and impressions caused him to lavish his verbal virtuosity on intangible areas of feeling and sensibility, making his diction more intangible, his sentences longer and more complex. In his own mind James *was* wrestling with matters of form, and he was doing so in what he con-sidered an aesthetically satisfying way; he was demonstrating how the artist could delve into the depths, attune himself to subtleties, and project those subtleties in language.

The idiosyncracies of the late style were compounded by the fact that James' magisterial manner and his increasing reputation as a "master" prevented anyone from seriously discussing with him how he sounded. Brother William is the only person I know who confronted James directly with the charge of obscurity, and of course, their rivalry, so well documented by Leon Edel, prevented Henry from even considering his brother's charges. James had no agent or editor who would discuss his style with him. His fellow artists, for their own reasons, did not bring up the matter of his style with him in person. When H. G. Wells made his criticism of James public in *Boon,* it was to attack James as the Culmination of the Superficial Type, his characters as "denatured" and "eviscerated," their motives only "a certain avidity and an entirely superficial curiosity."[36] Wells did not distinguish the intangibility and complexity of James' style from his overall method, and James' defense of his method was spirited and thorough: "It is art that *makes* life, makes interest, makes importance, for our consideration and application of these things, and I know of no substitute whatever for the force and beauty of its process."[37] In a sense, Wells granted James the assumption that his style was necessary for his subject matter, an assumption that James never questioned.

Thus I believe there is a perfectly good psychological explanation for the late style. That explanation does not account for the phrasing of particular passages, but it does account in general for the tone and "voice" of the style, for the magisterial persona: the artist as an explorer of psychological depths, the artist as oracle, the artist James wanted to be.

Despite our difficulty in coming to terms with James' "voice," it is his own—it is one he chose—and the difficulties with that voice are not James' but ours. The difficulty is with the limitations of our critical assumptions and methods.

5. *Style as Imitation*

Among all the ways in which we may explain the language of a literary work of art, the most common is not that the language is distinctive or that it expresses something about the author but that it is appropriate to the subject matter. In James' late style, therefore, the crucial question is this: are the extraordinary idiosyncrasies of the prose functional? That is, do the abstract diction, the complicated syntax, the parenthetical interruptions, the frequent use of expletives and passives imply a vision or a point of view that cannot be stated or expressed in any other way? Among literary critics the most common way of explaining the late style is by arguing that it "imitates" the subject matter. Here are a few examples:

"She had stature without height, grace without motion, presence without mass." The abruptness of this sentence [from *The Wings of the Dove*] may remind us that in the whole passage no sentence seems especially long, and that much of the force comes in short clauses: "She didn't judge herself cheap, she didn't make for misery." This is the Henry James whose later style is projecting the hard vitality of Kate with no fuss. (Charles R. Crow)[1]

[In attempting to determine the significance of the ellipses in "The Beast in the Jungle"] once again, with the best will in the world and after more than a little effort, the reader finds himself a bit lost in the portent of it all. But isn't that the point? Isn't it precisely the subtle, uncertain, heavy relationship between these two characters, shy and deferential and highly bred as they are, that James is depicting? Didn't the ends finally justify the means? (Seymour Chatman)[2]

[James' use of the past perfect tense] reproduces the way we perceive things at a 'great moment' when our attention is concentrated, with images coming to us overlapped. (Hisayoshi Watanabe)[3]

In James' sentence, the effort of holding the mind in suspense while each of the intervening modifications is gathered in, intensifies the force of the outcome and produces, in the end, a sense that not only the 'situation,' but the sentence itself has been saved. (Jane P. Tompkins)[4]

Each of these critical judgments asserts that James' late style imitates or reproduces something either in or outside the text. Crow claims that James' short sentences capture the "hard vitality" of Kate Croy in *The Wings of the Dove,* that long involved sentences would not suggest "hard vitality" as well as short ones. Chatman argues that the ambiguity of James' late style captures the uncertainty of the way the characters relate to one another, that explicit language would be less appropriate. Watanabe claims that James' use of tenses "reproduces" the way our minds work in certain situations, and Tompkins that the way we are forced to read James' heavily parenthetical syntax simulates the theme of "The Beast in the Jungle," that we as readers somehow resolve the uncertainty of James' sentences in the same way that the characters resolve their situation.

Judgments of this kind are common in criticism of James. In each case James' prose is supposed to "project," "depict," "reproduce," or "produce" something beyond its obvious meaning or referent. It is, however, often difficult to determine just what we mean when we say that a form of language can "project," "depict," "reproduce" or "produce" a quality, an attitude, or a meaning beyond its own referent. (I will use the generic term "imitate" for each of these verbs and what they seem to imply.) If we take imitation in its most literal sense, that of doing an activity in the manner of another, copying, or producing a representation, then the claim that style can imitate something else is clearly nonsense. As both Stanley Fish and Barbara Herrnstein Smith have gone to great pains to point out, there is no necessary correlation between a given stylistic feature and what it is supposed to imitate.[5] The abrupt sentences that describe Kate Croy do not copy or reproduce "hard vitality." The ellipses in "The Beast in the Jungle" do not copy or reproduce the relationship between Marcher and May. Past perfect tenses and parenthetical interruptions cannot reproduce anything, ex-

cept as a transcription of actual speech. What these various devices
do is evoke a certain response or association in the critic; the response
or association is entirely personal, private, subjective. Smith has a
formula for this kind of critical response: $S(R)X$; Analysis of $S \rightarrow X$. S
is a stylistic feature (Smith calls it the surface); X is what the style is
supposed to imitate (or in Smith's words "manifest"), and R is the
relation between the two. In stylistic criticism an analysis of S is supposed to lead to X, but R, the relationship between the style and what
it is supposed to imitate, is never specified; it is assumed.[6] As Smith
points out, this kind of argument is not unique to analyses of style; it
is, for example, the same kind of argument offered by critics who find
certain expressive qualities in literature:

> There is, of course, nothing surprising in the formula itself: it is a
> paradigm of many forms of analysis, from chemical to Freudian.
> Moreover, it is familiar from more traditional forms of literary
> analysis, particularly those performed over the past few decades
> by the legatees of the New Criticism, who commonly operated on
> the assumption that the "themes," "meanings," and "literary
> significances" of a work were "expressed" or "reflected" by its
> "form" or "language." In fact, the only thing that is surprising
> about the formula is how familiar it is, though the familiarity has
> been obscured by the new values given to its variables or, in
> some cases, by the new terms given to the old values. Thus,
> where it might, some years ago, have been image clusters or
> symbolism, it is now almost exclusively syntax. Or where it might,
> then, have been "sound patterns," it is now "phonological
> schemata."[7]

The relationship between a stylistic feature and what it imitates may
be conventional or personal, but it is never necessary. Most elementary
poetry texts, for example, cite onomatopoeia as a way in which sound
(S) clearly suggests what it refers to (X). But onomatopoeia does not
produce a copy; it produces a metaphor. An explosion from a faulty
exhaust pipe is not *bang*. The explosion sounds like *bang*. The sound
of curtains moving in the wind is not *swish*. The moving curtains sound
like *swish*. Many of the associations between onomatopoetic words
and what they suggest to us are so conventional that we may forget
for a moment that onomatopoeia is metaphoric. Equally metaphoric
are "phonetic intensives," syntactic patterning, any form of language

which suggests something beyond its literal sense or referent. Various critics such as Winston Weathers, Richard Weaver, and Louis Ceci, among others, have tried to demonstrate the "inherent qualities" of prose—that three-part compounds suggest certainty and didacticism, for example, or that complex sentences go "beyond simple perception" and illustrate "some sort of hierarchy, whether spatial, moral, or causal."[8] But the "inherent qualities" of these forms are determined by the meaning of the various elements in them. It is entirely a matter of personal opinion whether the three-part series "Bring a bat, a ball, and a glove to practice" implies certainty and didacticism more than, say, "Bring a ball and a bat to practice." It is equally a matter of personal opinion whether "The man who lives down the street is Mr. Smith" goes beyond simple perception or implies some sort of hierarchy more than, say, "That's Mr. Smith. He lives down the street." In each case we would have to know more about the critic, his background and presuppositions, and the circumstances in which he judged these expressions before we could decide the appropriateness of the judgments that they are, respectively, certain or hierarchical.

If, then, style cannot imitate, copy, or reproduce anything except metaphorically, what of all the critical claims that have been made in the name of mimesis? How are we to take them? I hope in the spirit in which they were intended: as a critic's personal sense of the appropriateness of that form of expression. To cite Barbara Smith once again, "An interpretation can be demonstrably 'wrong,' . . . only to the extent that it claims to be demonstrably 'right'."[9] And the interest we take in reading criticism is to see how the critic interacts with the text and to match our experience with his:

> A significant source of the pleasure and interest we take in our cognitive engagement with a poem is our presumption and projection (or hypothesizing) of the artist's "design," and a corresponding source of interest and pleasure for the spectator of such a reported engagement—or reenacted "game"—is precisely its consequent quality of *inter-play*. This is a quality, it might be added, that extends to the transaction between the interpreter and his own audience, since the latter will inevitably "match" his own experience of the work against that represented by the offered "reading," and, to the extent that the interpreter's game thus *itself* becomes an occasion for cognitive play, it serves an "aesthetic" function.[10]

We judge whether Crow, Chatman, Watanabe, and Tompkins are "right" by judging the appropriateness of the metaphors they use. It is not a matter of proof but of persuasion. Are the prose samples they cite representative of the claims they make? Are the metaphors they use convincing? In *The Wings of the Dove* does James' description of Kate Croy convey a sense of "hard vitality"? All we can do is read Crow's sample passages, note his metaphor, and nod in agreement or shake our head in disbelief. Do James' ellipses in "The Beast in the Jungle" suggest a heavy sense of portent? Do his past perfect tenses reproduce the way we perceive things at great moments? Do his parenthetical interruptions produce a sense of resolution? It depends. It depends on whether we see the point of the metaphor and leap to a similar conclusion. Indeed, a great deal of critical disagreement hinges on the not-so-simple matter of metaphor. One critic's metaphor is another critic's nonsense, and in response to James' late style the metaphors are many and often contradictory.

The most popular justification for James' late style is that the abstract diction and complicated syntax imitate the mind at work, that the style is a metaphor of mental process. In his book *Language Processing and the Reading of Literature*, George Dillon dramatizes the difficulty of this claim. He begins by quoting four critics: each critic justifies the prose he is analyzing with the argument that the prose imitates the mind thinking. Here are the quotations which Dillon cites:

> In his most characteristic writing, [he] is trying to render the transcendent life of the mind, the crowded composite of associative and analytical consciousness which expands the vibrant moment into the reaches of time, simultaneously observing, remembering, interpreting, and modifying the object of awareness. To this end the sentence as a rhetorical unit (however strained) is made to hold diverse yet related elements in a sort of saturated solution, which is perhaps the nearest that language as the instrument of fiction can come to the instantaneous complexities of consciousness itself. (Warren Beck)

> Not only is the reader forced to hold two or more possible sense resolutions in the forefront of his consciousness as he moves along but distinctions of time and space merge, qualitative differentiations are erased, and the neat compartmentalized autonomy of the conventional sentence is done away with. [He] simply presents a mass of experience in a lump, *now* as it enters the consciousness. (Robert Zoellner)

He designs a sentence whose very structure simulates the process of the mind, the manner in which we apprehend or perceive an idea. The dash and colon connect distinct ideas with an ease and fluency that belie the discreteness of the statement—they contribute an air of reality to the character's mental process. (Barry Menikoff)

But because [his] parentheses break into his sentences unpredictably they seem the product not so much of measured deliberation as of uncontrolled impulse. . . . Because [his] qualifications do not seem the result of any planned dislocation of syntax, they lend his prose an air of immediacy at the same time that they extend its analytic function. (Jane P. Tompkins)[11]

All four of these critics claim that the forms of language— the "related elements" of a sentence, the elements being lumped together, the punctuation, the parenthetical interruptions—can somehow render "the transcendent life of the mind," "consciousness," and "the process of the mind." Dillon's trick is that he has replaced the names of the writers being discussed with pronouns: these critics are not talking about the same person. The first two are discussing Faulkner; the last two are discussing James.

Dillon quickly points out that he has been somewhat unfair; the judgments of these critics are not all that much alike: "One can with effort discriminate between the passages on James and those on Faulkner: those on Faulkner describe experience only partly ordered or conceptualized, while those on James describe the process of conceptualization."[12] Still, Dillon's joke dramatizes the problem: when we claim that language can imitate mental life, just what are we claiming? The difficulty is brought into even greater relief by the fact that critics cannot agree on what James' late style is supposed to imitate. Some critics such as Ian Watt and Percy Lubbock argue that the late style imitates the thought of the characters; some critics such as Jane P. Tompkins argue that the late style imitates the thought of the narrator; and some critics such as Gordon O. Taylor argue that the late style imitates the life of the mind in general.[13] Still others, such as William Veeder, claim that the late style simulates the mental activity of readers as they read James' prose.[14] Thus, if we want to claim that James' late prose captures metaphorically some aspect of mental life, we need to clarify what is being imitated and we need to specify exactly how James does imitate it. Only then will the relation between the two be clear enough for us to decide whether the metaphor is effective, whether the various aspects of James' late style do functionally suggest certain kinds of mental operations.

In chapter 2 I dealt with the claim that any prose, James' included, "imitates" the mind of the reader or the mind in general. Critics who present models of the "ideal" or the "implied" reader only project the words of the text metaphorically into a scheme for how a reader might read the words of the text or how a mind might work to comprehend them. They generally offer no evidence that actual readers do in fact read according to their model or that the mind actually works in a way that a particular pattern in the text may represent metaphorically. Such claims are entirely hypothetical. However, the claim that style may "imitate" the thought of the characters or the thought of the narrator does not require evidence from outside the text: the claim is only that style is a metaphor for the artist's vision of mental life which is embodied in the text.

When critics claim that James' late style is an excellent imitation of mental processes, presumably they are claiming that it accurately reflects the view of the mind which was current around 1900, a view which James embodied in his work. According to Gordon Taylor, the way that American novelists conceived of the mind changed radically in the latter half of the nineteenth century:

> Roughly between 1870 and 1900 fictive psychology in the American novel undergoes a fundamental shift which may be summarized as follows. The basic view of the mind underlying the representation of consciousness in fiction moves away from a notion of static, discrete mental states requiring representational emphasis on the conventional nature of particular states, toward a concept of organically linked mental states requiring representational emphasis on the nature of the sequential process itself. At the beginning of the period, writers generally focus on a single level of rational awareness and develop it as conscious, logical introspection on the part of the character. As the period progresses, a broader and more complicated spectrum of psychological experience appears in their work, containing instinctual and sub- or semi-conscious levels or bands. At the close of the period, writers generally focus on links between interior process and exterior behavior in characters who are no longer introspectively aware of movement or change within their own minds. At the beginning the basic frame of reference for

psychological representation is abstractly moral; it assumes that mind is nonphysical, and measures the narrative importance of a mental event by its relation to the moral values and issues of the novel. At the end of the shift this frame of reference has become concretely environmental; mind is assumed to be physiological, and the development of narrative as well as the shaping of fictive issues depends on its response to environmental stimuli.[15]

At the end of this shift in the way artists conceived of the mind, consciousness became, in William James' metaphor, a stream often beyond our ability to control: it flows continuously with a tumble of associations, sometimes verbal, sometimes imagistic, occasionally rational but most often irrational; it is, in Taylor's words, "physiological" and responsive to "environmental stimuli," constantly reacting to and associating present stimuli with memories of things past. In *The Principles of Psychology* first published in 1890, William James characterized thought in a way which supports Taylor's thesis. James listed five major characteristics of thought:

1. Every thought tends to be part of a personal consciousness.
2. Within each personal consciousness thought is always changing.
3. Within each personal consciousness thought is sensibly continuous.
4. It always appears to deal with objects independent of itself.
5. It is interested in some parts of these objects to the exclusion of others and welcomes or rejects—chooses from among them, in a word—all the while.[16]

In arguing for a changing notion of "fictive psychology" in American literature, Taylor relies primarily on descriptions about novels which describe how the characters think. He does not cite many instances of characters in the process of thinking. However, Taylor's argument is bolstered by William Veeder, who does cite such passages, illustrating the common techniques for depicting mental life in the mid-1800s. According to Veeder, popular novelists of the period—novelists such as Charlotte Yonge in *The Heir of Radcliffe* and Susan Warner in *The Wide Wide World*—presented thought as transcribed speech. Here are some examples which Veeder cites from Yonge and Warner:

"All in vain, kind Charlie," said he to himself. (HR 2:31)

What was it? who was it?—The old newsman! Ellen was sure. Yes—she could see his saddlebags. This, then, must be Lady Keith!—but no sign of recognition? (WWW 355, 521)

Was it only an ordinary service of friendship? . . . Was it not a positive return of good for evil? Yes, evil! (HR 2:174)[17]

Veeder also shows that the popular novels of the period used a wider variety of techniques for illustrating mental action than Taylor gives them credit for. These techniques include the use of italics to make thought sound more colloquial and the ordering of perceptions sequentially. According to Veeder, these techniques are inadequate as metaphors for mental process because they do not capture the mind's ability to be open-ended and to generate thought, and although James imitated these techniques in his early fiction, he was able to transcend them in *The Portrait of a Lady* by establishing a new series of conventions for creating "the illusion of sustained mental process," a series of conventions he brought to perfection in the late style, especially in *The Ambassadors*.

The techniques which James developed, in Veeder's thesis, are these: the use of contrasting positive and negative assertions, the progression of thought from the general to the specific, and the contrasting of the literal and the metaphoric. Veeder is right, I think, in claiming that what James contributed to the depiction of mental life is a way of organizing, of patterning, the thought of his characters. What Veeder does not do is demonstrate how the late style depicts mental life differently from James' earlier styles and whether the abstract diction and the elaborate syntax do indeed contribute to our understanding of the inner life of his characters. This is what I propose to do now.

Before going any further, however, I think it would be helpful if I made more explicit and systematic the common literary techniques for depicting mental life in the middle of the nineteenth century before the advent of "stream of consciousness." Basically, at this time there were three kinds of techniques which a writer could rely on to show the mind at work: (1) the mode of presenting the thought—from more to less explicit, (2) the degree to which the narrator is present, and (3) patterns of thought and image. Geoffrey Leech and Michael Short have categorized the various modes of presenting thought this way:

1. Does she still love me? (Free Direct Thought: FDT)
2. He wondered, 'Does she still love me?' (Direct Thought: DT)

3. Did she still love him? (Free Indirect Thought: FIT)
4. He wondered if she still loved him. (Indirect Thought: IT)
5. He wondered about her love for him. (Narrative Report of a
   Thought Act: (NRTA)[18]

"He wondered, 'Does she still love me?' " pretends to be a direct transcription of thought, if thought could be made overtly verbal. "Does she still love me?" is called a free variation of Direct Thought because without the sentence tag it can be submerged in a passage of third-person narration:

> He walked the streets, consumed by the thought of her. She had ignored him so much lately. She refused to see him more than once a week. She was often busy when he called. But she is so beautiful, he thought; she is so perfect in every way. She can do no wrong. She is entitled to her own life. I must learn to accept that. Still, she seems so distant, so very far away. Does she still love me?

Indirect Thought removes the pretense of a direct transcription and merely approximates what a character is thinking: "He wondered if she still loved him." The free form of Indirect Thought can even more easily be submerged into third-person narration so that the Free Indirect form becomes almost indistinguishable from the narrator's voice:

> He walked the streets, consumed by the thought of her. She had ignored him so much lately. She refused to see him more than once a week. She was often busy when he called. But she was so beautiful, she was so perfect in every way. She could do no wrong. She was entitled to her own life. He had to learn to accept that. Still, she seemed so distant, so very far away. Did she still love him?

Narrative Report presents neither a direct transcription nor an approximation of a character's thought; it merely summarizes: "He wondered about her love for him."

Various critics have taken each of these modes to imply something different about the nature of thought; they have taken these modes as metaphors for mental life. Direct Thought, Indirect Thought, and Narrative Report, for example, use sentence tags—"he wondered"—to identify the character and to tell how he thinks. Sentence tags emphasize that it is indeed a character thinking, that thoughts do not exist independently of the person who makes them. If a prolonged passage depicting a character thinking is constantly interrupted by sentence tags, these critics argue, we as readers may find it more difficult to get a sense of the stream of thought: the constant interruptions to describe how the character is thinking or to comment on what he is thinking may remind us of the characters as fictive creatures subject to the author's will. Free Direct and Free Indirect Thought, on the other hand, lack sentence tags and thus, they may imply that thought flows continuously, free of a person who is thinking, or that the narrator has privileged access to the mental processes of his characters. Thus the degree to which a narrator intrudes on the thoughts of his characters has often been taken to imply something about the author's vision of mental reality.[19]

The degree to which the narrator intrudes on the thoughts of his characters has been a matter of considerable interest in criticism. Critics have paid special attention to the Free Indirect forms, tracing them back to Jane Austen and even Henry Fielding in the novel, although a consensus seems to be emerging that such forms did not become common until the mid-1800s.[20] Roy Pascal in *The Dual Voice* argues that Free Indirect Discourse increases the complexity of the novel:

> [Free Indirect Discourse] has thus meant a great enrichment of narrative style, since its use permits us to see the fictional characters moving not merely against the background of the narrator's consciousness, but within their own worlds of perception and understanding. . . . That is, the narrator is always effectively present in free indirect speech, even if only through the syntax of the passage, the shape and relationship of the sentences, and the structure and design of a story; usually, of course, he also appears as the objective describer of external events and scenes and of psychological processes, and as a moral commentator. Above all, perhaps, as the agency that brings multiple and complex events into relationship with one another and leads them to an end that establishes, even if without explicit comments, an all-embracing meaning.[21]

The way meaning is established in FID, of course, is through irony. The shift of a single indicator of tense from present to past may signal a shift in the status of an expression from one which the narrator wholeheartedly endorses and wishes us to endorse also, to one which only a character asserts and we are to question. Here is an example which Pascal cites from George Eliot:

> Celia thought privately, "Dorothea quite despises Sir James Chettam; I believe she would not accept him." Celia felt this was a pity. She had never been deceived as to the object of the baronet's interest. Sometimes, indeed, she had reflected that Dodo would perhaps not make a husband happy who had not her way of looking at things; and stifled in the depths of her heart was the feeling that her sister was too religious for family comfort. Notions and scruples were like spilt needles, making one afraid of treading, or sitting down, or even eating.[22]

Clearly, that *were* in the final sentence puts the sentiment in Celia's consciousness, but the tone is so closely related to the flow of the narration and to the narrator's own tone that we may pick up a sense of dry irony, of one person quoting another at her expense. James uses this technique with great success, as we shall see.

Free Indirect Discourse also allows the narrator to seemingly disappear from the narrative for extended periods of time, so that the irony is only cued by a shift in tenses, pronouns, adverbs of time, or any of a myriad of other indicators.[23] The freedom which this technique gives an author to render speech and thought and still comment on it is what so fascinates a wide variety of critics and may explain its increasing popularity during the nineteenth century as the novel became increasingly subjective and psychological. Indeed, Franz Stanzel has constructed an entire theory of the novel based on the degree of involvement of the narrator.[24]

In addition to the mode of presentation and the degree of involvement of his narrator, an author may render thought with various patterns of statement and image. Veeder maintains that a pattern of contrasting statements or images—from positive to negative, general to specific, literal to metaphoric—best suggests a mind at work, but there are certainly others that do so: chains of related images may capture the mind's ability to associate common elements or to leap from thought to thought and image to image; topic-comment form may suggest the mind's ability to contemplate a single subject for a time; indeed, even rational argument can illustrate that often we do verbalize mentally, if only for a short period, and therefore, at times Direct Thought is the most "mimetic" of the various modes of presenting thought.[25]

It is important to remember, therefore, that none of these techniques is inherently better than any other at capturing the flow of the mind. Rather, each of these techniques is a metaphor for a certain aspect of mental life, and the preference of a writer or critic for one technique over another will depend on his purposes; the aspect of the mind which he wants to emphasize, and his taste for metaphor.

These three techniques, then—various modes for presenting thought, various degrees of involvement by the narrator, and various patterns of thought and image—were the means at James' disposal to depict the life of the mind. As William Veeder, Roy Pascal, and others have pointed out, all of these techniques were in common use when James began his career as a writer. The question before us is how James assimilated them, used them to his own advantage, or even transcended them by creating techniques that had never been used before. This last claim, of course, is the common one used by critics to justify the late style.

In scrutinizing this claim I would like to illustrate how James' depiction of consciousness developed over the course of his career. Such a procedure will enable us to judge how a given technique functions in the late style in comparison with what has gone before, and it will highlight what is truly new in James' "major phase." In general, I hope to demonstrate the following about James' style:

—From his very first story James was concerned with point of view, with presenting information from a variety of points of view, and as early as his second story he depicted what Veeder calls "the illusion of sustained mental process."

—The techniques James used in his early stories to represent thought he used throughout his career; however, in *The Portrait of a Lady* he began to develop an elaborate way of presenting the mix of perception, feeling, and thought in his characters, and it is this elaborate patterning which he developed in the late style that makes his presentation of mental life unique.

—There is clearly no correlation between the complicated syntax and abstract diction of the late style and the thought of the characters; the idiosyncracies of the late style are in the language of the narrator, not in the thought of the characters. These idiosyncrasies cannot be justified by an appeal to imitation.

—Whether critics appreciate the late style for its patterning of consciousness is entirely a matter of taste. There is nothing inherently more "continuous" or "selective," nothing more able to capture life "mimetically" in James' late style than in his early style. In many ways, the late style cannot be justified aesthetically; it is simply the way James wrote.

In his very first story, "A Tragedy of Error," published in 1864, James showed an interest in third person limited narration, which would later become his trademark. The story is about a wife's attempt to arrange her husband's murder because she has taken a lover. Although the tale is told by an omniscient narrator, the narrator deliberately keeps his distance from his characters and often limits himself to the point of view of an observer on the scene. Leon Edel summarizes James' use of this limited focus:

Again and again it is not Henry James who sees what is going on but always someone else: "although to a third person it would have appeared . . ." "a wayfarer might have taken him for a ravisher escaping with a victim. . . ." On the way to the boat Hortense [the wife] walked "as if desirous to attract as little observation as possible . . . yet if for any reason a passerby had happened to notice her . . ." The third person, the observer, the wayfarer, the onlooker, the passerby—a cloud of witnesses—is wafted across the pages and their testimony is presented to the reader.[26]

In individual scenes James often describes the characters as if they were being seen by other characters in the scene. Here is the way the boatman, a potential accomplice, appears to Hortense Bernier, the woman who wants to do away with her husband:

Madame Bernier was plunged in a sidelong scrutiny of her ferryman's countenance. He was a man of about thirty-five. His face was dogged, brutal, and sullen. These indications were perhaps exaggerated by the dull monotony of his exercise. The eyes lacked a certain rascally gleam which had appeared in them when he was so *empresse* with the offer of his services. The face was better then— that is, if vice is better than ignorance. We say a countenance is "lit up" by a smile; and indeed that momentary flicker does the office of a candle in a dark room. It sheds a ray upon the dim upholstery of our souls. The visages of poor men, generally, know few alterations. There is a large class of human beings whom fortune restricts to a single change of expression, or, perhaps, rather to a single expression. Ah me! the faces which wear either nakedness or rags; whose repose is stagnation, whose activity vice; ignorant at their worst, infamous at their best! (TE, 32–3)

James signals the shift to a limited focus by saying that Madame Bernier was "plunged in a sidelong scrutiny of her ferryman's countenance," but he does not sustain that focus. By the time he switches to a judgment of the boatman's face, it is no longer clear whose point of view is being expressed, the narrator's or Madame Bernier's, and when he makes a sweeping statement about what "we say" and about "the visages of poor men" we are clearly back to the grand generalizations, not of Hortense but the omniscient narrator.

James uses the limited point of view most clearly with the maid, Josephine, who observes her mistress through a keyhole. At that moment we are privy only to what she sees:

Josephine stood a moment vexed, irresolute, listening. She heard no sound. At last she deliberately stooped down and applied her eye to the keyhole.

This is what she saw:

Her mistress had gone to the open window, and stood with her back to the door, looking out at the sea. She held the bottle by the neck in one hand, which hung listlessly by her side; the other was resting on a glass half filled with water, standing, together with an open letter, on a table beside her. She kept this position until Josephine began to grow tired of waiting. But just as she was about to arise in despair of gratifying her curiosity, madame raised the bottle and glass, and filled the latter full. Josephine looked more eagerly. Hortense held it a moment against the light, and then drained it down.

Josephine could not restrain an involuntary whistle. (TE, 28)

Although the narrator of "A Tragedy of Error" limits himself to the point of view of his characters, he almost never gets inside their minds. He stays deliberately outside and pretends to guess what their mental state is like:

"He [the boatman] evidently wished." (TE, 32)

"She [Hortense] walked as if desirous." (TE, 29)

"The man [the boatman] started, and stared a moment. Was it because this remark jarred upon the expression which he was able faintly to discern in her eyes?" (TE, 39)

When he does comment on the inner life of his characters, the narrator uses Narrative Report and never more than a sentence or two: "Josephine felt that she might not offer sympathy nor ask questions" (TE, 27). There is, however, one exception to James' general practice. At the end of the story he tells us what Hortense thought about as she waited for her lover:

"Is he a coward? is he going to leave me? or is he simply going to pass these last hours in play and drink? He might have stayed with me. Ah! my friend, you do little for me, who do so much for you; who commit murder, and—Heaven help me!—suicide for you! . . . But I suppose he knows best. At all events, he will make a night of it." (TE, 45)

This is, of course, Direct Thought. James uses those techniques which William Veeder has shown were common in popular nineteenth-century fiction: quoted questions and exclamations to show the mind grasping a topic with feeling, dashes and dots to show the mind leaping from thought to thought, in this case from thoughts of violence to those of grim hope. There is no sustained pattern of imagery. Hortense introduces the topic of what her lover will do that evening, goes over the possibilities, and jumps to the thought of what he might have done. That thought brings her no consolation and leads to what she has done for him— murder—and what she might still do—commit suicide. Then she leaps to her last hope, that her lover knows best and the evening might turn out all right. Despite the leaps of thought, the passage sounds like speech, a woman thinking aloud. The passage does, however, offer a metaphoric way of capturing a mind always changing, sensibly continuous, dealing with and choosing among objects. The dashes and dots especially mark the way Hortense leaps from thought to thought. As a metaphor for mental life, the passage is perhaps too explicit and too reasonable, lacking a way of capturing the mind's free association of object and image, thought and feeling, but it does at least suggest the movement of the mind from topic to topic.

With his second fiction, "The Story of a Year," published thirteen months after "A Tragedy of Error," James no longer restricts himself to outside appearances. "The Story of a Year" is overwhelmingly concerned with the mental life of its characters and adds one more convention to those James had already used, the use of Free Indirect Thought for an ironic interplay between the narrator and his characters. The year in James' title refers to the amount of time which Elizabeth Crowe must wait for her lover and fiancé, John Ford, to return from the Civil War. Lizzie is a weak shallow creature according to John and his mother, Mrs. Ford, and the omniscient narrator seems to agree:

> Lizzie lacked what is called a sense of duty; and, unlike the majority of such temperaments, which contrive to be buoyant on the glistening bubble of Dignity, she had likewise a modest estimate of her dues. Alack, my poor heroine had no pride! Mrs. Ford's silent censure awakened no resentment. It sounded in her ears like a dull, soporific hum. Lizzie was deeply enamoured of what a French book terms her *aises intellectuelles*. Her mental comfort lay in the ignoring of problems. She possessed a certain naive insight which revealed many of the horrent inequalities of her pathway; but she found it so cruel and disenchanting a faculty that blindness was infinitely preferable. She preferred repose to order, and mercy to justice. She was speculative, without being critical. She was continually wondering, but she never inquired. This world was the riddle; the next alone would be the answer. (SY, 65)

The focus and interest of the story is on how Lizzie will cope with the absence of her lover, whether she will be faithful and deal with the disapproval of Mrs. Ford, who happens to be not only her potential mother-in-law but her guardian as well. At Mrs. Ford's instigation— she is hoping that Lizzie will lose interest in her son—Lizzie goes to a party out of town and meets Robert Bruce, who is unusually attentive to her. By chance they meet at the train station on Lizzie's way home, and together they learn from a newspaper that John Ford's regiment has seen battle and John's name is on a list of the wounded. Lizzie, who is unconsciously attracted to Robert Bruce, is suddenly confronted with her duty to John, and the result is a dark night of the soul. Once on the train Lizzie is forced to deal with her feelings:

Lizzie felt conscious of a crisis which almost arrested her breath. Night had fallen at midday: what was the hour? A tragedy had stepped into her life: was she spectator or actor? She found herself face to face with death: was it not her own soul masquerading in a shroud? She sat in a half-stupor. She had been aroused from a dream into a waking nightmare. It was like hearing a murder-shriek while you turn the page of your novel. But I cannot describe these things. In time the crushing sense of calamity loosened its grasp. Feeling lashed her pinions. Thought struggled to rise. Passion was still, stunned, floored. She had recoiled like a receding wave for a stronger onset. A hundred ghastly fears and fancies strutted a moment, pecking at the young girl's naked heart, like sandpipers on the weltering beach. Then, as with a great murmurous rush, came the meaning of her grief. The floodgates of emotion were opened. (SY, 75)

This is hyperbole, and it is unclear whether James wants us to condescend to Lizzie because the rhetoric is excessive for her situation or whether he is simply inept at conveying the high tragedy of her feelings. Certainly the image of Lizzie's fears and fancies pecking at her heart like a sandpiper on a beach reduces her emotional state to an absurdity. Whether intentionally absurd or not, the hyperbole does call into question Lizzie's sincerity and force us as readers to evaluate it. So does the treatment of Lizzie's thought which immediately follows:

At last passion exhausted itself, and Lizzie thought. Bruce's parting words rang in her ears. She did her best to hope. She reflected that wounds, even severe wounds, did not necessarily mean death. Death might easily be warded off. She would go to Jack; she would nurse him; she would watch by him; she would cure him. Even if Death had already beckoned, she would strike down his hand: if Life had already obeyed, she would issue the stronger mandate of Love. She would stanch his wounds; she would unseal his eyes with kisses; she would call till he answered her. (SY, 75)

The tenses here reveal that this is Free Indirect Thought. Were the narrator addressing us directly, for example, he would have said, "Death may easily be warded off." And "she would" is clearly an object of "she reflected that." The FIT continues the ambiguous tone of the previous paragraph, what Roy Pascal calls "the dual voice." Had James consistently used Direct Thought—"I will go to Jack"—or Indirect Thought—"Lizzie decided that she would go to Jack"—Lizzie's decisiveness, her forcefulness, would have been clear. But by using FIT James calls into question her decisiveness and makes it seem hypothetical: "she would." In addition, by its nature FIT presents imagery ambiguously. Is Death beckoning and Life obeying the imagery of Lizzie's thoughts, or is it imagery imposed on Lizzie's thoughts, the narrator's method of interpreting and commenting on Lizzie's thoughts? From the passage itself, it is impossible to tell. In conjunction with the previous hyperbole, which is clearly the narrator's, the grand talk of Life and Death and Love strikes me as hollow. I attribute the imagery to the narrator; it is his way of ironically undercutting Lizzie's feeling and pointing out her dreamy romantic disposition. The extended parallelism also strikes me as ambiguous: it may be a way of capturing metaphorically the stream of Lizzie's thoughts, but the constant repetition of "she would" once again makes Lizzie sound excessive, as if she had to repeat these phrases to herself to give herself the courage of her convictions.

"The Story of a Year" is not limited to Lizzie's point of view. The narrator also assumes the point of view of John and Mrs. Ford and occasionally that of an anonymous spectator to the scenes containing the main characters: "Ford was lounging along with that calm, swinging stride which often bespeaks, when you can read it aright, the answering consciousness of a sudden rush of manhood. A spectator might have thought him at this moment profoundly conceited." (SY, 50)

Thus in his first two stories James used a repertoire of devices for dramatizing mental processes: a limited third-person point of view; the full range of direct and indirect modes for presenting thought, with various degrees of intrusion by the narrator, from direct first-person address to the subtle ironic commentary of Free Indirect Thought; conventional punctuation—dashes and dots, question and exclamation marks—to show the mind leaping from thought to thought; conventional imagery, clearly stated and, despite occasional leaps of thought, straightforwardly discursive and rational. What he did not do in these stories is impose a pattern on the imagery used by his characters to suggest the mind's ability to associate freely, and he did not discriminate among the kinds of mental activity in which his characters could engage. Leaps of thought are rare, and the characters sound in Direct Thought as if they were speaking aloud. But already, by using FIT, James has captured the ambiguity of what Paul Hernadi calls the "quasi-verbal" nature of thought.[27] The irony of James' early use of FIT, however, is rather thin: it has no larger philosophical purpose. The narrator presents the physical world as knowable, subject to his omniscient creation, as hard as the rock that Dr. Johnson kicked to refute Bishop Berkeley. The irony does not seriously question the perception or the intention of the characters. It merely mocks them.

The techniques I have mentioned became the standard means by which James dramatized mental operations throughout his career. They are the major techniques of the stories. Occasionally, in his novels James added patterns of imagery to suggest free association but not often. The novel in which he began to do so is *The Portrait of a Lady*.[28]

In that novel James greatly expands the techniques he has already developed, but only once—in the celebrated chapter 42 when Isabel looks back on her life with Osmond and realizes her ghastly mistake. Both before and after that scene James depicts mental life much as he has done before, using Narrative Report to summarize thoughts and occasionally Free Indirect Thought. Whenever he dramatizes Isabel's thoughts, as he does for example at the end of chapter 4, the end of chapter 21, the beginning of chapter 45, and the middle of chapter 49, James sets Isabel in a particular setting, summarizes her thoughts in Narrative Report, and constantly intrudes with comments and judgments by the narrator.

Chapter 42, despite its reputation, is no exception. James establishes the setting in the first paragraph, which is a continuation of the action from chapter 41. Osmond asks Isabel to try to influence Warburton to marry Pansy; then he leaves the room. Isabel dismisses the servant and sits thinking before the fire. Isabel's opening thoughts are presented no differently from James' previous practice. James uses a question, one which Isabel supposedly asks herself, and then a summary to illustrate her thought process:

> Was it true that there was something still between them [Isabel and Warburton] that might be a handle to make him declare himself to Pansy—a susceptibility, on his part, to approval, a desire to do what would please her? Isabel had hitherto not asked herself the question, because she had not been forced; but now that it was directly presented to her she saw the answer, and the answer frightened her. (354)

Isabel's question to herself, like the long list of questions that she asks herself shortly thereafter, is straight out of the popular literature of the late nineteenth century, as Veeder as shown. And after the list of questions James continues to summarize Isabel's thoughts and comment on them: "Isabel wandered among these ugly possibilities until she had completely lost her way . . . her soul was haunted with terrors which crowded to the foreground of thought as quickly as a place was made for them." (355)

And then suddenly James is off where he has not gone before, combining the direct presentation of the early stories with extended metaphors in a new and more dramatic way. In schematic form, what James does is this:

—He does not intrude with commentary or judgments once the illusion of thought begins. He tends to use fewer sentence tags and less Direct Thought, preferring instead to suggest the nature of the thought through Free Indirect Thought.

—Early he states what the characters are thinking about, and then he makes that thought more particular and concrete, often through metaphor. Making the thoughts of the characters more particular and concrete thus becomes a metaphor itself for a person coming to a realization of something she had in mind all along.

—He uses a chain of images or key words, repeated in synonyms and pronouns in successive sentences, to suggest the mind leaping from thought to thought on a single subject.

Here is Isabel coming to realize her deep distrust of her husband:

It was not her fault—she had practised no deception; she had only admired and believed. She had taken all the first steps in the purest confidence, and then she had suddenly found the infinite vista of a multiplied life to be a dark, narrow alley with a dead wall at the end. Instead of leading to the high places of happiness, from which the world would seem to lie below one, so that one could look down with a sense of exaltation and advantage, and judge and choose and pity, it led rather downward and earthward, into realms of restriction and depression where the sound of other lives, easier and freer, was heard as from above, and where it served to deepen the feeling of failure. It was her deep distrust of her husband—this was what darkened the world. (356)

The metaphor for Isabel's infinite possibilities before she married—a light, high, wide, and free vista—is sharply contrasted here with a metaphor for her life with Osmond—a dark, low, narrow, and restricted alley. To make these metaphors sound as if they were part of Isabel's thought, James uses no sentence tags. Instead, he integrates the metaphors into a direct third-person narration of what Isabel is thinking. The result is a very ambiguous tone. The imagery could be Isabel's or it could be the narrator's; the passage could be in Narrative Report or it could be in FIT. Personally, I find the imagery too literary for Isabel, so I ascribe it to the narrator. I find it more credible that the narrator would call Isabel's original intention "the infinite vista of a multiplied life," rather than Isabel herself; that the narrator would call her present situation the "realms of restriction and depression," rather than Isabel herself; that the narrator would describe Isabel's mental state in language which suggests how she might think of her position but not in the precise images of her actual thought.

Although this is primarily Narrative Report, the passage takes on life because of the way James balances sentences against one another and sets positives against negatives. The infinite vista becomes a narrow alley; it is not high and happy—it is low and restricted. The passage moves from a statement of what Isabel is contemplating—her lost direction—to a clearer specification of that direction. The passage states concretely what the direction used to be ("the infinite vista"), then what the direction is now ("the realms of restriction and depression"), and ends with a revelation of the cause of her lost freedom: her distrust of her husband.

This representation of thought lasts only for a short time, after which James intrudes with a judgment of Isabel's character: "Suffering, with Isabel, was an active condition." (356) Then James is off again, and except for an occasional sentence tag to remind us that it is Isabel who is thinking, he does not intrude again for six long pages. Most of this extended passage is discursive and in FIT; it is remarkably similar to the earlier stories, different only in length. And as before, the FIT is ambiguous: "She had had a more wondrous vision of him fed through charmed senses and oh such a stirred fancy!—she had not read him right." (357) Is this Isabel referring to her own senses as "charmed" and her own fancy as "stirred"? Is it her "oh" and her exclamation? Or are these the narrator's way of describing her rather ironically? A later metaphor is equally ambiguous:

> She had felt at the same time that he was helpless and ineffectual, but the feeling had taken the form of a tenderness which was the very flower of respect. He was like a sceptical voyager strolling on the beach while he waited for the tide, looking seaward yet not putting to sea. It was in all this she had found her occasion. She would launch his boat for him; she would be his providence; it would be a good thing to love him. And she had loved him, she had so anxiously and yet so ardently given herself. (357–8)

Are the images of beach and boat Isabel's, or are they the narrator's way of summarizing how Isabel thought of Osmond? Dorrit Cohn believes they are Isabel's thoughts:

> The simple past of the second sentence can be understood as a normal lapse from the pluperfect of the narrated memory. But the conditional of the third [sic] sentence ("she would . . . she would . . . it would") can only be a narrated monologue of Isabel's past illusions about the future: a future that, at the moment of her retrospection, already lies in her disillusioned past. We have here, to be precise, a narrated fantasy within a narrated memory. Translation into direct quotations at both time levels yields: (She thought:) "It was in all this I found my occasion. I thought to myself: 'I will launch his boat for him; I will be his providence; it will be a good thing to love him.' And I have loved him. . . ." To complicate matters further, the preceding sentence in simple past ("He was like a sceptical voyager . . ."), which on first reading looked like a lapsed pluperfect, can now be interpreted with equal validity as a narrated monologue to the second degree, nested *within* the narrated memory: (She thought: "I thought: 'He is like a sceptical voyager.' "[29]

This is an interpretation which makes the passage seem like a series of Chinese boxes. I do not think it obvious, however, that this passage is in FIT. I find it equally plausible that the passage is in Narrative Report and that the metaphors are the narrator's. The first sentence is clearly in Narrative Report, and we could interpret the rest of the passage as an object of "she had felt that": she had felt that "she would launch

his boat for him," she had felt that "she had loved him." In this interpretation the second sentence would be a "lapsed pluperfect," a way
of continuing the force of the narrative without repeating *had*. For us
to accept Cohn's interpretation we would have to believe that Isabel
said something like this to herself, "I will launch his boat for him; I
will be his providence; it will be a good thing to love him," a complexity
of metaphor I find it easier to associate with the narrator than with
Isabel.[30]

In any case James' technique of using an ambiguous mixture of
Narrative Report and Free Indirect Thought reaches its height in this
well-known passage:

> She could live it over again, the incredulous terror with which she
> had taken the measure of her dwelling. Between those four walls
> she had lived ever since; they were to surround her for the rest of
> her life. It was the house of dumbness, the house of suffocation.
> Osmond's beautiful mind gave it neither light nor air; Osmond's
> beautiful mind, indeed seemed to peep down from a high small
> window and mock at her. Of course it was not physical suffering;
> for physical suffering there might have been a remedy. She could
> come and go; she had her liberty; her husband was perfectly
> polite. He took himself so seriously; it was something appalling.
> Under all his culture, his cleverness, his amenity, under his good-
> nature, his facility, his knowledge of life, his egotism lay hidden
> like a serpent in a bank of flowers. She had taken him seriously,
> but she had not taken him so seriously as that. How could she—
> especially when she knew him better? She was to think of him as
> he thought of himself—as the first gentleman of Europe. (360)

This lyrical outburst is unique in the Jamesian canon. Nowhere else
does the narrator absent himself for such a long period of time or
eliminate the use of sentence tags. The passage announces a theme—
Isabel's terror—and proceeds to specify more concretely the nature of
that terror, both what it is and what it is not, and its ultimate cause.
The images and metaphors here are of lightness and darkness, breadth
and restriction, height and depth—to suggest the way the mind comes
back again and again to certain motifs. The passage is held together
by a closely linked chain of images which are repeated over and over
as if Isabel's mind were jumping from one idea to the next with one
recurrent image as a link: the house, Osmond's mind, his seriousness.
The repetition of these images and the qualities associated with them

is the primary way in which James makes Isabel's terror more specific and concrete. For example, the nature of Osmond's seriousness is specified by listing all of the qualities which hide his egotism: his culture, his cleverness, his amenity, his good nature, his facility, his knowledge.

And once again the tone is ambiguous. The Narrative Report sweeps us along, presenting the gist of what Isabel is thinking in the language of the narrator but with occasional hints of Free Indirect Thought. Whether we attribute these hints of FIT to Isabel will depend on how we interpret the quality of her mind. Is it likely that Isabel would refer to her home as "the house of darkness, the house of dumbness, the house of suffocation" or to Osmond as "a serpent in a bank of flowers"? These expressions may be the lyricism of Isabel's thoughts or the narrator presenting a metaphor for how a person might think in such a situation. If we interpret these expressions as Narrative Report, occasional phrases and sentences will still sound like FIT: "She had taken him seriously, but she had not taken him so seriously as that. How could she—especially when she knew him better." The question here signals FIT, the narrator mimicking how Isabel would ask herself, "How could I continue to take him seriously—especially when I knew him better." Narrative Report blends so well with FIT here that at times it is impossible to tell the mode of presentation. I find the last sentence, for example, very difficult to interpret. Is this the narrator telling us that Isabel, after she had decided not to take Osmond so seriously, eventually came to think of him as "the first gentleman of Europe"? Or is this Isabel thinking what she eventually came to think. I can't tell.

In any case, the intensity of the passage does not last long. In the next paragraph James returns to more traditional forms of presenting mental operations. Sentence tags return: "Isabel saw that"; "she knew that"; "she had an undefined conviction that." The narrator begins to intrude once more: "of which I have spoken," "as I have intimated," "Poor Isabel." Then, almost at the end of the chapter, James very briefly drops Isabel altogether and slips into Ralph's point of view: "Ralph smiled to himself, as he lay on his sofa, at this extraordinary form of consideration; but he forgave her for having forgiven him" (364). Nevertheless, in the last lines of the chapter James returns to the setting as if he had been inside Isabel's head all along:

> For herself, she lingered in the soundless saloon long after the
> fire had gone out. There was no danger of her feeling the cold;

she was in a fever. . . . When the clock struck four she got up; she was going to bed at last, for the lamp had long since gone out and the candles burned down to their sockets. (364)

Thus *The Portrait* is both a continuation and a breakthrough. The novel continues James' use of the third- person limited point of view— and not just Isabel's: the novel expresses the point of view of almost every major character at one time or another. It also continues the use of the full range of mental representation but especially Narrative Report and Free Indirect Thought, with a strong presence by the narrator. What *The Portrait* adds to James' repertoire of metaphors for mental process is a way of patterning imagery to capture the leap of the mind from topic to topic and a way of showing how the mind dwells on certain themes by association. These conventions are in many ways no better than James' original ones—the use of dots and dashes to signal abrupt changes in thought—but many critics have found them more eloquent.

And so about twenty-five years after *The Portrait* and with almost forty years of experience writing fiction, concerned from the very beginning with the third-person limited point of view and the presentation of mental life, James evolved his celebrated late style. In the novels he wrote at the beginning of this late period, James often used a first-person narrator and limited the point of view exclusively to the narrator. I'm thinking of "The Turn of the Screw" and *The Sacred Fount*. But in the great novels of the late period—*The Ambassadors*, *The Wings of the Dove*, and *The Golden Bowl*—James relied exclusively on the third-person limited point of view. In the stories he also uses both points of view. The very fact that we recognize something similar in the styles of all these novels and stories indicates that what they have in common may tell us about something broader than the mental life of the characters: the style may be simply the narrator's voice. Whether in first-or third-person, that voice is the one which James adopted late in his career as a public voice, a voice that we need not necessarily associate with James himself or his personality but which dominates the novels and stories in spite of the fact that we cannot associate it with any particular personality.

This larger issue is crucial to critics such as Franz Stanzel, who argue that James' late work is figural, an example of the modernist trend toward unidentified or—in Stephen Daedalus' term—Godlike narrators.[31] It is crucial to Stanzel's argument that we identify the late style with the characters. If we do not, if we become overly aware of the narrator talking, Stanzel's main example of a "Godlike" narrator, indeed his entire theory, becomes questionable.

I suppose by now I have tipped my hand. When I read the late James, all I hear is that distinctive voice. Except for the dialogue—and often not even then—I do not hear Strether or Kate Croy or the Prince, or even the nameless narrator of *The Sacred Fount*, a novel written in the first person. So when I read about the thoughts of James' characters in these books, I am all too aware that I am reading the words of a person some distance from the action, viewing it, describing it, indeed *creating* it, as he goes along, and what I am reading is the narrator's interpretation of those thoughts. In those rare cases when I do become aware of Free Indirect Thought, I am so conscious of how the narrator is imposing his language on the thought of the characters that I have great difficulty realizing how the transcription could be even an approximation of what the characters are thinking.

There are, I think, two reasons for this. First, much more than in the early style James relies on sentence tags to name the kind of thought his characters are engaged in. Seymour Chatman, building on the work of Michael Shriber, classifies James' mental verbs into four groups—perception, precognition, cognition, and belief.[32] I do not want to differentiate these kinds of verbs—the title of each group fairly indicates what sort of mental activity is represented in each group—but I do wish to emphasize Chatman's point, that James is engaged in discriminating among the kinds of thought his characters are engaged in. To do so he must label each kind of thought, and so in the late novels and stories there is rarely an extended passage without the intrusion of the narrator as there was in *The Portrait of a Lady*. Secondly, much more than previously James is trying to blend exterior action, perception, and the various kinds of thought into a single "impression." To do so he must constantly refer to what is going on outside his characters, what they see, then tell how they perceive it and how they think about it. Paradoxically, to capture the sense of a total impression in the third person James is forced to rely even more on his narrator's voice to blend the exterior action with perception and thought. And when that voice has all the idiosyncrasies of James' late style, the characters themselves tend to get lost in the narrator's manipulation of them. James' use of Narrative Report so dominates his descriptions and his blending of exterior action, perception, and thought is so thorough that traditional distinctions among the modes of thought break down. Usually, Narrative Report is exclusively in the language of the narrator and Indirect Thought, or even Free Indirect Thought, is supposed to take on some semblance of the language of the characters. But in the late style the language of the narrator in Narrative Report is so dominant that even passages which are cued as Indirect Thought or Free Indirect Thought sound like the narrator. Let me illustrate.

In the eighth book of *The Ambassadors* there is a scene which closely monitors Strether's reactions to a very limited range of outside activity: the scene in which, after greeting Sarah, Mamie, and Jim at the train station, Strether rides away in a cab with Jim. The scene begins with the setting and the announcement that Strether is "crowded" with impressions:

> It was in the cab with Jim that impressions really crowded on Strether, giving him the strangest sense of length of absence from people among whom he had lived for years. Having them thus come out to him was as if he had returned to find them; and the droll promptitude of Jim's mental reaction threw his own initiation far back into the past. Whoever might or mightn't be suited by what was going on among them, Jim, for one, would certainly be: his instant recognition—frank and whimsical—of what the affair was for *him* gave Strether a glow of pleasure. "I say, you know, this *is* about my shape, and if it hadn't been for *you*—" so he broke out as the charming streets met his healthy appetite; and he wound up, after an expressive nudge, with a clap of his companion's knee and an "Oh you, you—you *are* doing it!" that was charged with rich meaning. Strether felt in it the intention of homage, but, with a curiosity otherwise occupied, postponed taking it up. (AMB, II, 78)

Here is what the narrator tells us about Strether's mental state: impressions crowd him and give him "the strongest sense of length of absence," Jim's reaction to Paris reminds Strether of his first acquaintance with Paris and makes it seem a long time ago; Jim's recognition of his situation gives Strether "a glow"; Strether feels in Jim's expression a kind of homage. With all this naming of how the particular circumstances impress Strether, what do we learn of what he is thinking? Is any of this in Free Indirect Thought? I detect only one clause which might represent what Strether is thinking: "Whoever might or mightn't be suited by what was going on among them, Jim, for one, would certainly be." This may be what Strether is thinking as reported in FIT, but because the clause flows so unnoticeably into the surrounding

Narrative Report, it is very difficult to distinguish from the narrator's voice. It has no special diction or punctuation to mark it. In fact, the elaborating clause after the colon *is* in Narrative Report and tells us what gave Strether a glow of pleasure in language which is clearly the narrator's: this is probably not Strether saying to himself that Jim's recognition was frank and whimsical but the narrator omnisciently telling us how Jim affected Strether. "Frank and whimsical" may be terms which Strether would use to describe Jim if he were talking to himself, but buried in a sentence of Narrative Report, we have no way of knowing whether Strether used these words or not.

The very next sentence of the passage brings out all of the issues raised by the late style. It is an example of Indirect Thought: "What he was asking himself for the time was how Sarah Pocock, in the opportunity already given her, had judged her brother—from whom he himself, as they finally, at the station, separated for their different conveyances, had had a look into which he could read more than one message." (AMB, II, 78) The question is whether this example of IT is phrased as Strether would say the words to himself, whether the diction and syntax are the character's or the narrator's. Here is the thought in direct form: "In the opportunity already given her, how has Sarah Pocock judged her brother Jim—from whom I myself, as we finally at the station separated for our different conveyances, had a look into which I can read more than one message." Put in this way, of course, the thought is absurd. If Strether were talking to himself he would not refer to Sarah as Sarah Pocock but merely as Sarah and he would not have to remind himself of all the circumstances surrounding the ambiguous look from Jim. He would simply think something like this: "How does Sarah judge her brother?" This passage, then, is a prime example of how artificial any method of presenting thought really is, even the indirect methods. Indirect Thought in this case is certainly no more accurate a metaphor for mental life that Direct Thought. The delayed syntax—that most famous characteristic of the late style—is the narrator's, a way for him to provide more information for the reader who does not know the circumstances under which Strether received Jim's look.

Narrative Report, then, a description of the characters' thought in the language of the narrator, is the dominant technique of the late style. This is not to say that James totally avoids other techniques. In fact, in the second paragraph after the passage I have just quoted, he clearly uses FIT to record Strether's reaction to Sarah's appreciation of Chad:

Ah how much, as it was, for all her [Sarah's] bridling
brightness—which was merely general and noticed nothing—
would they work together? Strether knew he was unreasonable; he
set it down to his being nervous: people couldn't notice
everything and speak of everything in a quarter of an hour.
Possibly, no doubt, also, he made too much of Chad's display.
Yet, none the less, when, at the end of five minutes, in the cab,
Jim Pocock had said nothing either—hadn't said, that is, what
Strether wanted, though he had said much else—it all suddenly
bounced back to their being either stupid or willful. It was more
probably on the whole the former; so that that would be the
drawback of the bridling brightness. Yes, they would bridle and
be bright; they would make the best of what was before them, but
their observation would fail; it would be beyond them; they
simply wouldn't understand. Of what use would it be then that
they had come?—if they weren't to be intelligent up to *that* point:
unless indeed he himself were utterly deluded and extravagant?
Was he, on this question of Chad's improvement, fantastic and
away from the truth? Did he live in a false world, a world that had
grown simply to suit him, and was his present slight irritation—in
the face now of Jim's silence in particular—but the alarm of the
vain thing menaced by the touch of the real? Was this
contribution of the real possibly the mission of the Pococks?—
had they come to make the work of observation, as *he* had
practised observation, crack and crumble, and to reduce Chad to
the plain terms in which honest minds could deal with him? Had
they come in short to be sane where Strether was destined to feel
that he himself had only been silly? (AMB, II, 80–81)

Notice here how the FIT blends in with the Narrative Report. After the
first sentence, which is clearly in FIT, we arrive at "Strether knew he
was unreasonable," which is not an explicit statement of what Strether
is thinking (which would be "I know I am unreasonable") but a summary
of a thought deeper than words, signaled by the word *knew*. The clause
after the colon is clearly in FIT, however: if it were the narrator making
a general announcement the verb would be *can't*. The next sentence
continues in FIT, and then we return to Narrative Report: Strether would
not tell himself that Jim had not said what he wanted him to. Beginning
with "It was more probably on the whole the former" we are back in
FIT, and we continue in it for the rest of the passage.

A number of things need to be said here. One is that the final series of questions in FIT is merely a shade away from questions in DT, the technique which Veeder associates with the hackneyed popular fiction of the period. According to Veeder we simply do not talk to ourselves this way, and therefore the technique is artificial, if not dishonest. Putting the questions into the third person helps a little, I suppose, because the third-person does not pretend to be a direct transcription, but when the questions pile up as they do here, there is obviously no attempt at verisimilitude. James is merely using a straightforward and time-honored convention. Another thing that needs to be pointed out is more important to my case. Notice the way the delayed syntax and certain other locutions peculiar to the narrator occur even in FIT: "Ah how much, as it was, for all her bridling brightness"; "Possibly, no doubt, also, he made too much." This sort of carryover from the narrator's voice to Strether's thought is what I am referring to when I say that in the late style I have difficulty hearing anything but the narrator's voice. In addition, some of the vocabulary strikes me as a little odd for Strether. I wonder, for example, whether "bridling brightness," despite the fact that it occurs in FIT, is a phrase that Strether would invent or play around with as he does in this passage. I associate "bridling brightness" with the narrator and his attempt to interpret Strether's thought for us. What happens to certain critics when they read this or similar passages is that they take the narrator's voice—his tics and quirks—and project it onto the characters. For some reason, I cannot do that—all I hear is that omniscient narrative voice, directing and commenting.

The way in which James imposes his narrative voice on the thought of his characters is clearly illustrated by his use of metaphors in *The Golden Bowl*. In that novel James presents an extended metaphor to illustrate Maggie's mental processes, and he blends Narrative Report and Free Indirect Thought so completely that it is not clear whose metaphor is being elaborated—Maggie's or the narrator's. Here, for example, is part of Maggie's famous interior monologue, which opens book 4:

> This situation had been occupying, for months and months, the
> very centre of the garden of her life, but it had reared itself there
> like some strange, tall tower of ivory, or perhaps rather some
> wonderful, beautiful, but outlandish pagoda, a structure plated
> with hard, bright porcelain, coloured and figured and adorned, at
> the overhanging eaves, with silver bells that tinkled, ever so

charmingly, when stirred by chance airs. She had walked round and round it—that was what she felt; she had carried on her existence in the space left her for circulation, a space that sometimes seemed ample and sometimes narrow; looking up, all the while, at the fair structure that spread itself so amply and rose so high, but never quite making out, as yet, where she might have entered had she wished. (GB, II, 3)

We may not be able to differentiate the narrator's voice from Maggie's thought in this passage while we are reading it, but when the passage is over, James clearly labels the metaphor as a device for "representing" Maggie's thought:

If this image, however, may represent our young woman's consciousness of a recent change in her life—a change now but a few days old—it must at the same time be observed that she both sought and found in renewed circulation, as I have called it, a measure of relief from the idea of having perhaps to answer for what she had done. The pagoda in her blooming garden figured the arrangement—how else was it to be named?—by which, so strikingly, she had been able to marry without breaking, as she liked to put it, with her past. (GB, II, 4–5)

If the pagoda metaphor is an authorial device to "represent" Maggie's thought, then Maggie may not be thinking about a pagoda. The image of the pagoda may be a way for the narrator to dramatize how elaborate and artful are Maggie's ruminations. Maggie's thoughts may be *like* a pagoda. On the other hand, James does say that Maggie looked at the pagoda, that she "walked round and round it—that was what she felt."

James uses the same device to illustrate Maggie's thoughts about Charlotte in chapter 40. There Maggie thinks of Charlotte as trapped in a glass cage, and just as he did with the pagoda figure, James labels the glass metaphor as an authorial invention:

Charlotte was hiding neither pride nor joy—she was hiding humiliation; and here it was that the Princess's passion, so powerless for vindictive flights, most inveterately bruised its tenderness against the hard glass of her question.

Behind the glass lurked the *whole* history of the relation she had so fairly flattened her nose against it to penetrate—the glass Mrs. Verver might, at this stage, have been frantically tapping from within, by way of supreme, irrepressible entreaty. . . . She could thus have translated Mrs. Verver's tap against the glass, as I have called it, into fifty forms; could perhaps have translated it most into the form of a reminder that would pierce deep. (GB, II, 329)

Here the words "as I have called it" clearly indicate that the metaphor is the narrator's way of describing Maggie's thought, that the metaphor is not in Free Indirect Thought but Narrative Report.

To me, then, the main ways in which the late style depicts mental process is not through diction and syntax, which I associate with the narrator, and not through the use of FIT, which James has been using since his second story, but through the blending of Narrative Report and other modes of presenting thought and through a mix of perception, cognition, and feeling artfully arranged.

The most celebrated passage in the late style is an example of this sort of patterning: it is the recognition scene in *The Ambassadors*, when Strether comes upon Chad and Madame de Vionnet boating on the river. The patterning is of larger sections of discourse than the sentence, and so it is unrelated to syntax. In this scene James describes what Strether sees and then what Strether infers from what he sees in order to simulate—the argument goes—a dawning awareness. Now I agree that James handles the scene masterfully, but what he does is rather straightforward: he describes what happens in some detail and has Strether try to puzzle out what the actions mean, thereby delaying the moment when Strether cries ah-ha! David Lodge summarizes the workings of the scene this way:

> His method is, characteristically, to impose logical order—and therefore chronology—upon mental processes that are intuitive and partly synchronized. He spreads out lineally the overlapping responses and actions of the characters involved so that we are able to distinguish clearly between them and follow the sequence of cause and effect.[33]

Here is the passage we are considering:

> What he [Strether] saw was exactly the right thing—a boat advancing round the bend and containing a man who held the paddles and a lady, at the stern, with a pink parasol. It was suddenly as if these figures, or something like them, had been wanted in the picture, had been wanted more or less all day, and

had now drifted into sight, with the slow current, on purpose to fill up the measure. They came slowly, floating down, evidently directed to the landing-place near their spectator and presenting themselves to him not less clearly as the two persons for whom his hostess was already preparing a meal. For two very happy persons he found himself straightway taking them—a young man in shirt-sleeves, a young woman easy and fair, who had pulled pleasantly up from some other place and, being acquainted with the neighborhood, had known what this particular retreat could offer them. The air quite thickened, at their approach, with further intimations; the intimation that they were expert, familiar, frequent—that this wouldn't at all events be the first time. They knew how to do it, he vaguely felt—and it made them but the more idyllic, though at the very moment of the impression, as happened, their boat seemed to have begun to drift wide, the oarsman letting it go. It had by this time none the less come much nearer—near enough for Strether to dream the lady in the stern had for some reason taken accounts of his being there to watch them. She had remarked on it sharply, yet her companion hadn't turned around; it was in fact almost as if our friend had felt her bid him keep still. She had taken in something as a result of which their course had wavered, and it continued to waver while they just stood off. This little effect was sudden and rapid, so rapid that Strether's sense of it was separate only for an instant from a sharp start of his own. He too had within the minute taken in something, taken in that he knew the lady whose parasol, shifting as if to hide her face, made so fine a pink point in the shifting scene. It was too prodigious, a chance in a million, but, if he knew the lady, the gentleman, who still presented his back and kept off, the gentleman, the coatless hero of the idyll, who had responded to her start, was, to match the marvel, none other than Chad. (AMB, II, 256–57)

The sequence presented in this scene is almost one of stimulus and response, as shown in figure 6. This pattern of stimulus and response is done entirely in Narrative Report. I detect no Free Indirect Thought, the narrator borrowing Strether's voice, except perhaps in the expression "It was too prodigious, a chance in a million." The overall pattern, together with the narrative voice, blurs the distinctions between perception and thought: the passage flows easily from "what he saw" to an inference based on that perception, "it was suddenly as if," back

What Strether Sees	What Strether Infers
—the boat, a man paddling, a woman with a pink parasol	—they complete the picture
—the boat comes toward the landing	—they are the people for whom the landlady is fixing a meal
—the man is in shirt-sleeves and the woman is easy and fair	—they are happy, expert, familiar and frequent
—the boat drifts wide; the man lets it go; (the woman says something to the man)	—she has "taken account of him"

Fig. 6.   Stimulus/response in the recognition scene.

to further perception and thought—"further intimations," "he vaguely felt"—which culminate in the final revelation: "if he knew the lady, the gentleman . . . was . . . none other than Chad."

Now there is no doubt that in this scene James is depicting Strether's progressive realization that it is in fact Chad and Madame de Vionnet before him, but whether the syntax in some way "mimes" Strether's progress depends on our taste for metaphors. Generally, the sentences increasingly specify what is stated earlier. The fourth sentence, for example, asserts that Strether finds the couple happy and then gives a possible reason why they might be happy: "[They] had pulled pleasantly up from some other place and, being acquainted with the neighborhood, had known what this particular retreat could offer them." Most of the parenthetical information of the paragraph comes at the end of sentences and then to make a previous observation more specific or concrete. The only sentence that is unusually delayed is the last one. The realization which this sentence describes is that if the woman is Madame de Vionnet, then the man must be Chad. Were this sentence somehow a transcription of reality, the realization would be instantaneous. James, however, captures this instant realization in two rather long sentences:

> He too had within the minute taken in something, taken in that he knew the lady whose parasol, shifting as if to hide her face, made so fine a pink point in the shining scene. It was too prodigious, a chance in a million, but, if he knew the lady, the gentleman, who still presented his back and kept off, the gentleman, the coatless hero of the idyll, who had responded to her start, was, to match the marvel, none other than Chad. (AMB, II, 257)

A number of facts are asserted here: that Strether recognizes the lady, that she shifts her parasol as if to hide her face, that the gentleman must be Chad. Everything else in the passage we already know, so it cannot be that James is piling on detail to "mime" the simultaneity of impressions. We have already been told and Strether has already noted that the gentleman is without a coat and that he had responded to the lady's start. The only reason for repeating this information now—along with "to match the marvel," a repetition of "a chance in a million"— is to build the sentence to a climax. The repetition strikes me as a rhetorical device, plain and simple, and because of its length, in one sense at least, as far from an imitation of an instantaneous impression as language can get. If we do take these two long periodic sentences as a metaphor for a sudden realization, we are indulging a taste for metaphor in which the form of any sentence could capture the instantaneous.

If, then, James does capture Strether's consciousness at work in this passage, it is less through the elaborate syntax—or only in the sense that all diction and syntax can capture consciousness at work—than it is through the overall patterning of the passage and the way James blurs the distinction among the kinds of mental activity—perception, inference, the manifold forms of cognition.

So far I have relied primarily upon *The Ambassadors* to illustrate my contention that the late style captures the illusion of mental process in a different way than is commonly asserted. But if we look at other work in the late style, we will see that James uses his public style for other uses than mental activity and even with first-person narrators. Here, for example, is the opening of "In the Cage," written in 1898, in which the diction is remarkably concrete and the mental life of the heroine is only occasionally referred to:

> It had occurred to her early that in her position—that of a young person spending, in framed and wired confinement, the life of a guinea-pig or a magpie—she should know a great many persons without their recognizing the acquaintance. That made it an emotion the more lively—though singularly rare and always, even then, with opportunity still very much smothered— to see anyone come in whom she knew outside, as she called it, anyone who could add anything to the meanness of her function. Her function was to sit there with two young men—the other telegraphist and the counter-clerk; to mind the "sounder," which was always going, to dole out stamps and postal-orders, weight letters,

answer stupid questions, give difficult change and, more than anything else, count words as numberless as the sands of the sea, the words of the telegrams thrust, from morning to night, through the gap left in the high lattice, across the encumbered shelf that her forearm ached with rubbing. This transparent screen fenced out or fenced in, according to the side of the narrow counter on which the human lot was cast, the duskiest corner of a shop pervaded not a little, in winter, by the poison of perpetual gas, and at all times by the presence of hams, cheese, dried fish, soap, varnish, paraffin, and other solids and fluids that she came to know perfectly by their smells without consenting to know them by their names. (ITC, 367–68)

This passage does incorporate elements of the cage girl's perception ("It had occurred to her"; "outside, as she called it") and it suggests her attitude in certain adjectives ("answer stupid questions, give difficult change"), but mostly it is exposition, setting the scene for what is to follow. James uses elaborate syntax here, basically, to describe the girl's situation; the syntax does not capture the girl's thoughts as much as it merely enumerates the monotonous details of her dreary life.

And here is the first-person narrator of *The Sacred Fount*, who speaks the same language as the anonymous narrator of the great novels:

There was a general shade in all the lower reaches—a fine clear dusk in garden and grove, a thin suffusion of twilight out of which the greater things, the high tree-tops and pinnacles, the long crests of motionless wood and chimnied roof, rose into golden air. The last calls of birds sounded extraordinarily loud; they were like the timed, serious splashes, in wide, still water, of divers not expecting to rise again. I scarce know what odd consciousness I had of roaming at close of day in the grounds of some castle of enchantment. I had positively encountered nothing to compare with this since the days of fairy-tales and of the childish imagination of the impossible. *Then* I used to circle round enchanted castles, for then I moved in a world in which the strange "came true." It was the coming true that was the proof of the enchantment, which, moreover, was naturally never so great as when such coming was, to such a degree and by the most romantic stroke of all, the fruit of one's own wizardry. I was positively—so had the wheel revolved—proud of my work. I had thought it all out, and to have thought it was, wonderfully, to have brought it. Yet I recall how I even then knew on the spot that there was something supreme I should have failed to bring unless I had happened suddenly to become aware of the very presence of the haunting principle, as it were, of my thought. This was the light in which Mrs. Server, walking alone now, apparently, in the grey wood and pausing at the sight of me, showed herself in her clear dress at the end of the vista. It was exactly as if she had been there by the operation of my intelligence, or even by that—in a still happier way—of my feeling. My excitement, as I have called it, on seeing her, was assuredly emotion. Yet what *was* this feeling, really?—of which, at the point we had thus reached, I seemed to myself to have gathered from all things an invitation to render some account. (SF, 128–29)

Here the narrator moves from the awareness of concrete details into the realm of pure imagination in a way which is almost a satire of the typical mental life of James' characters—from the recollection of clear dusk and high trees and loud bird calls (at the time in the past of the story he is telling) to a remembrance of childhood fantasies (remembered now at the time the narrator is writing) and back to a recollection of how childhood fantasies may have been operating at that earlier twilight time when Mrs. Server may have appeared merely because he wanted her to, because his imagination demanded it. Both diction and syntax are typical of the late style, as are the shifts in time and the report of thought in retrospect, but the mental life they are used to illustrate is so refined that the narrator has to stop himself, lost as he is in wonder that reality could so closely correspond to his desires, and he must reassure himself that his excitement is really emotion.

Whether he is using a first- or third-person narrator, whether he is describing mental life or not, James uses variations of his public style after the mid-1890s. It is a style distinctively his, but whether it serves an aesthetic function, we have cause to wonder. I do not think that James' diction and syntax, especially his use of expletives *it* and *there* and many of his awkward parenthetical interruptions, can be appropriately ascribed to the mental processes of the characters. Certainly, they do not strike me as contributing to a notion of mental life as any more selective or continuous, any more of an approximation of how the mind flows and leaps than the more straightforward reveries of Lizzie Crowe in "The Story of a Year," written forty years earlier. And I can think of no other justification. They are simply mannerisms, the way James wrote. I do, however, think that the patterns with which James presents his characters thinking are an effective and eloquent metaphor for mental life. James' genius is shown in the way he describes the personal nature of experience, the way reality is only known by and filtered through a point of view, and he conveys that great truth through his manipulation of point of view and his patterning of perception and thought. The abstract diction and convoluted syntax are largely irrelevant to that purpose. Many of James' late mannerisms may be justifiable, but the argument that the diction and syntax "mime" mental process is not the way to do it.

6. *Conclusion*
The Limits of Stylistic Criticism

I hope by now my main point is clear and persuasive: in many ways James' late style transcends the traditional ways we have of explaining style. It is not conventionally expressive of certain aesthetic traits such as eloquence, and in those passages we could cite as examples of eloquence, we have to account for other characteristics we can only call dense, clumsy, turgid. Neither is James' style clearly expressive of certain aspects of his personality: he could write informally and directly in his letters and journals, and the published style is so various that we cannot correlate any particular features with any subject matter or theme. The persona James did project is open to a variety of interpretations but does not seem to be guided by a larger aesthetic or rhetorical purpose. Finally, we cannot justify the late style thematically or functionally by arguing that it reflects the way in which the characters think or the way we carry on mental processes generally. There is no significant correlation between James' use of any particular kind of diction and syntax and the mental life of his characters. Nor is there any significant correlation between his use of any particular kind of diction and syntax and any model we have for mental process.

Of course, the difficulty of explaining James' late style has not stopped critics from finding a great deal in James' prose, and that is perfectly reasonable. Almost all of James' critics are aesthetic monists who are sensitive to the nuances of language and dedicated to the notion that a difference in "affect," however subtle, is a difference in "meaning." The best of the critical reactions to James' late work are triumphs of tenacity and ingenuity, and my inability to accept them is, in a very real sense, not their fault. These critics clearly recognize certain aspects of James' language and have plausible reasons for why James would want to write that way. They present their case with a great deal of evidence and clear argumentation, and that is all anyone can expect. My failure to be convinced can be explained very simply by the principles of critical argument I have already discussed: the very selective nature of our critical attention. We notice and explain and justify what we can, most often using the conventional arguments of expression and imitation and most often focusing on a very few features in a very small sample. Carried to its logical conclusion, however, the assumption that we can explain any given feature of a text leads to the notion that we ought to be able to explain, at least theoretically, every feature of a text, that there is an aesthetic or thematic reason for every pause and comma in an artist's use of language. I find this assumption questionable. The forms of language are too conventional, the human mind too spontaneous, for us to provide a word-for-word, syllable-by-syllable explanation of why one way of saying something is superior or "more meaningful" than another, for in a real sense there is no explanation. In a very real sense, there is no explanation for the particular form of the sentence I am writing right now. These are simply the words that came to mind, and when I go back to edit, as I am doing now, I may find things to alter or expand upon, I may find some unwanted alliteration or awkwardness that I want to delete, I may be delighted with a particularly felicitous phrase and decide to leave it in. But to argue that the very form of these sentences reflects some qualities of expressiveness or that they imitate a theme (This sentence is going on and on, and after all, I am talking about the process of composition) is decidedly a matter of after-the-fact conjecture, a matter of the conventions of criticism. (What about that alliteration *delete— delighted—decide*? Does it sound tinny? It was certainly not intentional, but I rather like the play of *delete—delight* and I will leave it in. In a sense, then, the alliteration is now intentional.) We read literature to give our imagination and intellect free rein, to discover and explain what we can, but what we can explain is only a very small part of a text, the part that caught our attention, the part that yielded itself to some possible explanation. It seems to me that the greater part of a text, what we refer to as its style, is much more the result of a happy accident than it is the product of conscious control, and our critical explanations tell us more about the imagination and the intellect of the critic than they tell us about how a given passage of prose came to be or why it is the way it is.

To dramatize the limitations of stylistic criticism, I would like to show how even the close analysis of a great critic can fail to account for the most fundamental aspects of style and how stylistic criticism may tell us more about the interests and taste of the critic than about the style in question. The critic I have in mind is Ian Watt, whose analysis of the first paragraph of *The Ambassadors* is the best example of stylistic criticism I know. Watt's thesis is straightforward: James' style is "a supremely civilized effort to relate every event and every moment of life to the full complexity of its circumambiant conditions."[1] And the primary way in which James does this, according to Watt, is by presenting simultaneously Strether's consciousness and the narrator's. The narrator in effect "translates what [Strether] sees into more general terms, makes the narrative point of view both intensely individual and yet ultimately social."[2] Watt argues, then, that every aspect of James' style is significant because each feature contributes to this larger purpose of presenting a dual consciousness and the complexity of life's "circumambiant conditions." For this larger purpose James' style is "an amazingly precise means of expression."[3] Here is the first paragraph of *The Ambassadors*, which Watt attempts to explain in these terms:

1. Strether's first question, when he reached the hotel, was about his friend; yet on his learning that Waymarsh was apparently not to arrive till evening he was not wholly disconcerted. 2. A telegram from him bespeaking a room "only if not noisy," reply paid, was produced for the inquirer at the office, so that the understanding they should meet at Chester rather than at Liverpool remained to that extent sound. 3. The same secret principle, however, that had prompted Strether not absolutely to desire Waymarsh's presence at the dock, that had led him thus to postpone for a few hours his enjoyment of it, now operated to make him feel he could still wait without disappointment. 4. They would dine together at the worst, and, with all respect to dear old Waymarsh—if not even, for that matter, to himself—there was little fear that in the sequel they shouldn't see enough of each other. 5. The principal I have just mentioned as operating had been, with the most newly disembarked of the two men, wholly instinctive—the fruit of a sharp sense that, delightful as it would be to find himself looking, after so much separation, into his comrade's face, his business would be a trifle bungled should he simply arrange for this countenance to present itself to the nearing steamer as the first 'note' of Europe. 6. Mixed with

everything was the apprehension, already, on Strether's part that it would, at best, throughout, prove the note of Europe in quite a sufficient degree. (AMB, I, 3)

In this paragraph Watt finds five major characteristics: (1) a preference for nontransitive verbs (14 passive, copulative, or intransitive uses, as opposed to six transitive ones), (2) many abstract nouns (four abstract nouns as the subjects of main clauses, while only three clauses have concrete or personal subjects), (3) much use of "that"-clauses, (4) elegant variation to avoid piling up personal pronouns and adjectives, and (5) the presence of a great many negatives or near-negatives. Here is Watt's explanation of the first sentence, which can serve as an example of the way he explains James' use of nontransitive verbs and abstract nouns in general:

> Consider the first sentence. The obvious narrative way of making things particular and concrete would presumably be "When Strether reached the hotel, he first asked 'Has Mr. Waymarsh arrived yet?' " Why does James say it the way he does? One effect is surely that, instead of a sheer stated event, we get a very special view of it; the mere fact that actuality has been digested into reported speech—the question 'was about his friend'— involves a narrator to do the job, to interpret the action, and also a presumed audience that he does it for: and by implication, the heat of the action itself must have cooled off somewhat for the translation and analysis of the events into this form of statement to have had time to occur. Lastly, making the subject of the sentence "question" rather than "he," has the effect of subordinating the particular actor, and therefore the particular act, to a much more general perspective: mental rather than physical, and subjective rather than objective; "question" is a word which involves analysis of a physical event into terms of meaning and intention: it involves, in fact, both Strether's mind and the narrator's.[4]

From James' use of abstract nouns and nontransitive verbs, his extensive use of *that*-clauses, the "elegant variation" of pronouns, and the use of negatives necessarily follows:

> The number of "thats" follows from two habits already noted in the passage. "That" characteristically introduces relative clauses

dealing not with persons but with objects, including abstractions; and it is also used to introduce reported speech—"on his learning that Waymarsh"—not "Mr. Waymarsh isn't here".

Reported rather than direct speech also increases the pressure toward elegant variation: the use, for example, in sentence 1 of "his friend," where in direct speech it would be "Mr. Waymarsh" (and the reply—"*He* hasn't come yet"). In the second sentence— "a telegram . . . was produced for the inquirer"—"inquirer" is needed because "him" has already been used for Waymarsh just above; of course, "the inquirer" is logical enough after the subject of the first sentence has been an abstract noun—"question"; and the epithet also gives James an opportunity for underlining the ironic distance and detachment with which we are invited to view his dedicated "inquirer," Strether.

This abundance of negatives has no doubt several functions: it enacts Strether's tendency to hesitation and qualification; it puts the reader into the right judicial frame of mind; and it has the further effect of subordinating concrete events to their mental reflection; "Waymarsh was not to arrive," for example, is not a concrete statement of a physical event: it is subjective—because it implies an expectation in Strether's mind (which was not fulfilled); and it has an abstract quality—because while Waymarsh's arriving would be particular and physical, his *not* arriving is an idea, a non-action.[5]

Watt does a superb job of providing a theoretical rationale for the style of this passage. His reasons for the five characteristics he notices in the passage are plausible to me and ones which any writer might very well assent to. There are, however, two main limitations to Watt's argument, the same limitations which I think apply to most stylistic criticism to date. First of all, Watt's most successful explanations for James' late style are sufficiently general that they account not only for James' style but for a wide range of possible styles, and secondly, when Watt does try to account for more exact wording in the text, when he claims that "it can be proved that all or at least nearly all of the idiosyncrasies of diction and syntax in the present passage are fully justified by the particular emphases they create," his explanations become less convincing and more a matter of personal taste.

Consider for example Watt's explanation of the first sentence: that reported speech is necessary to convey the dual perspective of both the narrator and Strether and that the abstract subject is necessary to convey a sense of "mental perspective." By Watt's own criteria James still could have written these variations of his first sentence: (1) Having reached the hotel, Strether asked about his friend. (2) When he reached the hotel, Strether' first question was about his friend. The first variation is still reported speech involving a narrator "to do the job, to interpret the action," although it is still not sufficiently "mental" for Watt because of the active verb. The second variation restores the abstract subject of the original, but it maintains a more common word order—the subordinate clause first rather than in the middle of the sentence. Why the noun *question* is "a word which involves analysis of a physical event into terms of meaning and intention" more than the verb *asked* is something I do not know. In any case, James could have met Watt's criteria for the first sentence by writing the second variation. But Watt goes on:

> In the first part of the opening sentence, for example, the separation of subject—"question"—from verb—"was"—by the longish temporal clause "when he reached the hotel," is no doubt a dislocation of normal sentence structure; but, of course, "Strether" must be the first word of the novel: while, even more important, the delayed placing of the temporal clause, forces a pause after "question" and thus gives it a very significant resonance.[6]

These judgments, of course, are entirely personal, a matter of taste. *Strether* need not be the first word of the novel to satisfy Watt's explanation that the passage illustrates a dual consciousness at work or that it captures the full complexity of circumambiant conditions. Neither does the embedded clause have to produce "a very significant resonance" for Watt's explanation to be persuasive. In both of these instances Watt likes the wording of the original, and whether we accept his judgment or not will depend entirely on whether our taste is similar to his, whether we think novels such as the *The Ambassadors* should begin with the name of their main character or whether we think embedded clauses resonate more than introductory ones.

Or consider Watt's discussion of the negatives in the passage. Watt asserts that "the abundance of negatives" "*enacts* Strether's tendency to hesitation and qualification," another example of the notion that

James' style imitates mental life. At the opening of the novel, however, Strether is not as hesitant as he was before: his past ambiguous desire to see Waymarsh "now operated to make him feel he could wait without disappointment." And the issue of what is being enacted raises the problem of the degree to which James is dramatizing Strether's mental processes here. Watt treats the passage as if it were in Free Indirect Thought, so that every negative is an example of Strether's consciousness at work. I think Watt is right to attribute much of sentence 4 to Strether's thought: "dear old Waymarsh" is clearly an expression which Strether would use. But sentence 3, which contains so many negatives, is just as clearly in Narrative Report, and the negatives reflect the speech of the narrator; they do not enact Strether's hesitation at all. Watt goes on: the negatives put the reader into "the right judicial frame of mind"— an assertion which we have seen is entirely hypothetical—and they aid in "subordinating concrete events to their mental reflection":

> "Waymarsh was not to arrive," for example, is not a concrete statement of a physical event: it is subjective—because it implies am expectation in Strether's mind (which was not fulfilled); and it has an abstract quality—because while Waymarsh's arriving would be particular and physical, his *not* arriving is an idea, a non-action. More generally, James' great use of negatives or near-negatives may also, perhaps, be regarded as part of his subjective and abstractive tendency: there are no negatives in nature but only in the human consciousness.[7]

I find this a curious argument because both the perception of a physical event and the contemplation of possibilities are mental. What Watt seems to be asserting is that a preponderance of negatives in a style conveys a sense of mental subjectivity better than a number of positive assertions. This is an assertion about what language can express, and as such it depends upon the associations a critic makes between a certain feature of a text and something outside the text. I can only say that Watt may associate negatives and subjectivity, but I do not.

Later Watt again relies on the argument of expressive language: parts of the paragraph suggest to him an "echoing doom" and "a fine full fatal note," and the placement of a single adverb, *throughout*, can produce "no limit to the poignant eloquence." To which I can only respond that all of these qualities went by me when I read the passage the first time, and even now I have difficulty accepting them: they seem excessive somehow, an attempt to turn this opening paragraph into something more dramatic than it really is.

Watt also continues to rely on the notion of style as imitation; for example, when he argues that grammatical forms can indicate the themes of the novel:

> James, we saw, carefully arranged to make "Strether's first question," the first three words; and, of course, throughout the novel, Strether is to go on asking questions—and getting increasingly dusty answers. This, it may be added, is stressed by the apparent aposiopesis: for a "first" question when no second is mentioned, is surely an intimation that more are—in a way unknown to us or to Strether—yet to come. The later dislocations of normal word-order already noted above emphasise other major themes; the "secret principle" in Strether's mind, and the antithesis Waymarsh-Europe, for instance.[8]

I find Watt's attempts to explain the placement of every word and the form of every sentence increasingly arbitrary. It strikes me that any first word to a novel can be justified in one way or another, that all clauses produce a resonance of one kind or another, that any form of language can suggest mental life or "enact" some form of mental activity, that all language can express in some sense joy or sadness, freedom or doom. The difficulty with these very personal associations, as Stanley Fish has pointed out, is that there seem to be no constraints on the number or kind of associations a critic can make. Theoretically, everything is related at some level of abstraction to everything else. I admire Watt's ingenuity, but I find many of his associations completely unconvincing. This criticism does not apply, however, to his overall rationale for the passage. I think that a great deal of James' language can be explained by the notion that it presents a dual consciousness at work and that it captures the full complexity of life's circumambiant conditions. The difficulty with such general rationales, however, is that they explain any number of versions of the same passage. As an example I offer the following revision, which Watt's rationale explains admirably but which is more explicit and in more normal sentence order than James' original: (1) When he reached the hotel, Strether's first question was about his friend; yet upon learning that Waymarsh was apparently not going to arrive until evening, he was content. (2) The clerk produced a telegram from Waymarsh asking for a room "only if not noisy," reply paid, and Strether immediately understood that their plan to meet at Chester rather than Liverpool was still in effect. (3) Earlier Strether had not been certain that he wanted to meet Waymarsh at the dock, and so he had postponed his arrival for a few hours; now, however, his old uncertainty operated to make him feel he could still wait without disappointment. (4) They would dine together at the worst, and with all respect to dear old Waymarsh Strether had little fear that they should not see enough of each other thereafter. (5) Strether's uncertainty had been wholly instinctive—the fruit of his sharp sense that his business would be a trifle bungled, should he simply arrange for Waymarsh to present himself to the nearest steamer as the first "note" of Europe, no matter how delightful he would find his comrade's face after so much separation. (6) Mixed with everything ahead was Strether's apprehension that Waymarsh would, at last, throughout, prove the note of Europe in quite a sufficient degree.

The difference between this revision and the original is, it seems to me, less a matter of "meaning" than it is a matter of taste, although I must admit that in the revision Strether's uncertainty is much more clearly in the past. I do think, however, that Watt's overall rationale for James' paragraph applies equally to the revision.

I argued in the second chapter that the great majority of our explanations of style seem to be limited to two conventions: hypotheses about authorial intent and hypotheses about "affects" on readers. And I argued that both of these conventions have little relationship to empirical reality; that is, we have no way of knowing an author's "real" intent, and when authors do tell us what they had in mind we often feel that they do not understand their own work very well; likewise, when we claim that a given passage of prose has a certain effect, we are usually being entirely hypothetical: we do not cite our own experiences or anyone else's as evidence for such a claim; we offer the effect as one possibility, one way in which that prose once may have affected someone or may affect someone in the future.

Increasingly, it seems to me, we are reaching a consensus about the nature of reading, in which, to use Kathleen McCormick's words, "textual regularities must be regarded as intersubjectively verifiable rather than as 'objective.' Reading is a learned behavior, and it is learned in social and linguistic contexts that are always changing."[9] Because reading is learned in different ways in different circumstances, the way we read will always vary from reader to reader, and in the case of one reader, individual readings will vary from circumstance to circumstance in a complex interplay of context and convention. But because we share a common form of neural engineering and because we often learn common strategies of reading, to say nothing of "common knowledge," this range of experience does not result in anarchy or solipsism, only in acknowledged differences. We recognize our experience in the experience of others; we recognize the keen perception and the good sense in the interpretations of others. And our ability to convince others of the good sense in our own interpretations is contingent upon our ability to recognize these differences and appeal to common strategies and experiences. The more we become aware of how and why we use a particular critical method or a particular critical metaphor, the more we can clarify both the nature of literary criticism and the nature of reading itself. Although the process of reading will not "explain" a particular interpretation, the more we make the process explicit, the more context our readers will have for understanding why we interpret a text in a particular way.

For most criticism of style the natural end and extension of language really does border on nonsense, an area of the mind full of conjecture and possibility unrelated to actual intentions and "real" effects, an interior world of shifting impressions and "felt" intuitions beyond words, beyond language itself, in which convention and context work together to produce an interpretive text that must itself be interpreted with all the care we devote to literary texts. But I do not think that the criticism of style is any less important for bordering on the nonsensical. Clearly, Watt's explanation for the first paragraph of *The Ambassadors* makes good sense as an overall rationale: it accounts for the passage in some detail, and it gives good reasons for why James may have wanted to write the way he did, consciously or not. As such it helps us to confront not only James' language but all language, to play with possible meanings and explore the limits of what language can and ought to mean. If I disagree with many of Watt's rationales for particular readings, that is to be expected. At some point, at a different point in every text, all explanations break down, and we must confront the fact that language is spontaneous and springs from the deepest wells of our consciousness, that for many things we say and write, no matter how carefully crafted, there is no aesthetic or thematic reason: these are simply the words that sprang to mind. Sooner or later all stylistic criticism must confront that limit, and with James, it seems to me, we confront it sooner than with many other writers. James' style is simply the way it is, impervious to explanations and rationales; it transcends traditional forms of analysis and justification.[10] We can either stand in awe of it and try as we can to make sense of it, or we can dismiss it out of hand as nonsense.

The most striking thing that I have discovered in studying James' late prose is how much of it can be explained by a simple rhetorical device—periodicity (contrary to James' general reputation for writing "loose" or convoluted prose). Overwhelmingly, James' sentences and paragraphs are delayed in order to put a striking image or metaphor, a sudden realization or the point of a slowly evolving awareness at the end.[11] Notice how all of the sentences in the first paragraph of *The Ambassadors* are generally periodic and end either with a short predicate or with a more specific elaboration of a previous clause. Often this technique is breathtaking, as it is at the end of "The Beast in the Jungle" or in the description of Densher's vigil in *The Wings of the Dove*. But over the course of a story or a novel, as the periodic sentences roll on and on, I find myself becoming numb to them. My concentration flags, and sometimes, even after twenty minutes, I find myself reading entire pages and discovering, as I turn the page, that I have no idea of what I just read. And so I have to go back and read the passage again, slowly, carefully, parsing out meaning line by line. I do not find this an enjoyable way to read novels, and the rewards, despite the claims of James' greatest admirers, are less than those of great poetry.

And yet. And yet. There is that voice, that voice that echoes in my mind, a voice, on the one hand, as ponderous and majestic as a proclamation from Olympus, and on the other, as colloquial and careful as a man at the fireplace of his club, brandy and cigar in hand, telling a story to his fellows and wanting to get all the nuances of his story just right. I cannot justify that voice. It is simply there, like the proverbial mountain. Or better yet, as a significant body of work. I believe that after a time a writer who takes his job seriously and achieves something of the magnitude of *The Portrait of a Lady*—and that novel leaves me spellbound in admiration every time I read it—such a writer has earned a right to my respect whether I "appreciate" some of his work or not. I have read enough of James by now to realize that the effort to read him is worth it in the long run, even though I must exert myself in short bursts and often find myself lost and confused along the way.

I believe that by the time he came to write in the late style, James was entitled to any voice he chose. And despite my failure to recognize the poetry in every pause and the significance of every slangy phrase, I have no doubt whatsoever, even as I reread a passage for the fourth time just to get the gist, that I am reading the language of a master.

Appendix A
Appendix B
Notes
Bibliography
Index

Appendix A
The Variety of James' Fiction

Of course, I cannot deny that on the average—for great expanses of prose—James' fiction exhibits the characteristics we often associate with his late style. But within the confines of about three hundred words, which may be the limit of our ability to note and defend stylistic choices by close analysis and to present an argument based on that analysis, James' style exhibits considerable variety. The shifting distribution of features we associate with James' style is a clear illustration of what makes the development of a concept of style so complex. Just as a child may develop a concept of, say, a dog primarily by observing the spaniels, terriers, and German shepherds in the neighborhood and still be able to recognize a Russian wolfhound as a dog, even though he has never seen one before in his life, so too we may recognize James' style, even though the passage we recognize contains very few of the features we associate with James. To demonstrate the point more fully, I have analyzed four additional passages from *The Wings of the Dove*, all about three hundred words long, three chosen at random and one purposely chosen because it seems to be the exception to the rule. I chose the random passages by dividing the thirty-seven chapters of the novel by four and taking the middle narrative paragraph from each of the chapters one-fourth, one-half, and three-fourths of the way through the book; that is, chapter 3 of book 4, chapter 3 of book 6 and chapter 1 of book 9. (WOD, I, 187–88; II, 37–38; II, 239–40) By narrative paragraphs I mean paragraphs not dominated by dialogue or inserted in the middle of dialogue to describe either speaker or listener. I numbered the paragraphs with no dialogue, divided the number of the last paragraph by two, rounded upward for fractions, and chose that middle paragraph for analysis. The fourth passage, the one deliberately chosen because it does not seem particularly Jamesian, is from the second chapter of book 9, the eighth paragraph. (WOD, II, 263–64)

The results can be seen in table 3. Even among the random passages there is a great deal of variety. Average sentence length ranges from 34.5 to 53.3 words per sentence. Intangible nouns are the subjects of main clauses from 30.8 percent to 63.6 percent of the time. Verbs of mental action occur in main clauses from 23.1 percent to 30 percent of the time. I found the parenthetical interruptions almost impossible to distinguish as either common or odd (Is a transition such as *however* inserted after the subject of a sentence a parenthetical interruption or not?), so I merely counted every break in the normal word order set off by commas or dashes, but not transitions or inversions, such as introductory adverbials. Even so, many of my identifications are clearly arbitrary, and so the numbers of this feature are suspect. I counted, for example, "they had clearly, in talk, in many directions, proceeded to various extremities" as an interruption, but not "the quantity her new friend had told her might have figured as small, as smallest, beside the quantity she hadn't." In any case, either because of the sloppiness of my methods or in spite of them, for this one feature there was some consistency: I counted 13, 11, and 13 parenthetical interruptions, respectively, in the random passages, which ranged from 311 to 320 words each. The remaining features were very infrequent and, I suspect, of negligible importance in identifying the passages in question. It seems to be the combination of the features, however various, and the subject matter which makes the passages recognizably Jamesian.

One further remark: just how useless stylistic features can be in determining the nature of a prose passage is illustrated by the fourth selection. Everything in the passage is what Densher perceives and thinks, and yet the percentage of intangible nouns and verbs of mental action is small. Mental activity can be presented concretely and with active verbs. The presence or absence of any given set of features, in and of itself, does not tell very much about what is going on in the language under consideration.

Table 3
A Comparison of Passages from *The Wings of the Dove*

Feature	Random Passage 1	Random Passage 2	Random Passage 3	Selected Active Style
Average Sentence Length				
No. of Sentences	9	9	6	16
No. of Words	313	311	320	299
Words/Sentence	34.8	34.5	53.3	18.7
Nominals as Subjects of Main Clauses				
Active Agents (%)	46	69	36	52
No./Total	6/13	9/13	4/11	17/33
Intangible Nouns (%)	53.9	30.8	63.6	36.4
No./Total	7/13	4/13	7/11	12/33
Deictic Pronouns (%)	15	0	27	12
No./Total	2/13	0/13	3/11	4/33
Expletives *it/there* (%)	23	15	18	9
No./Total	3/13	2/13	2/11	3/33
Actor-Agent in Oblique Position Sentences				
No./Total	4/13	1/13	2/11	4/33
Verbs of Mental Action				
Verbs in Main Clauses (%)	30	23.1	27.3	14.7
No./Total	5/15	3/13	3/11	5/34
Past Perfect Tenses (%)	26.7	0	27.3	17.6
No./Total	4/15	0/13	3/11	6/34
Loose Sentences with Weak Conjunctions Sentences				
No./Total	1/9	2/9	0/6	2/16
Semicolons followed by Loose Supplemental Phrases or Clauses	0/9	1/9	1/6	0/16
Parenthetical Interruptions	13/9	11/9	13/6	3/16
Ambiguous Conditionals	0/9	0/9	0/6	0/16
Logical Terms Words				
No./Total	4/313	1/311	0/320	0/299
Colloquial Two-Word Verbs Verbs in Main Clauses				
No./Total	2/15	0/13	0/11	0/34
Italicized Words of Relation Words				
No./Total	0/313	2/311	1/320	1/299

Appendix B
The Variety of James' Writing as a Whole

The data for table 2 in chapter 4 are based on the following passages:

Letters

To Mrs. de Navarro	(LET, 328)
To Sidney Colvin	(LET, 330–32)
To Edmund Gosse	(LET, 332)
To Henrietta Reubell	(LET, 333–35)
To H.G. Wells	(LET, 335–36)
To C.E. Norton	(LET, 337–39, up to the postscript)

The letters are dated from October 13 to November 24, and in the Lubbock volume are in this order. I omitted a letter in the form of a tale dated October 13.

Notebooks

All of the entries for October 5, November 11, and November 12 (NOT, 293–97). I omitted a list of prospective names for characters on page 295.

"The Saint's Afternoon"

The first four sections (SA, 345–355)

"The Future of the Novel"

The first four paragraphs (FN, 30–36)

"The Two Faces"

All of the narrative paragraphs, those not dominated by dialogue
(TF, 239, 241, 244–45, 248, 251–53)

I have already noted the difficulty of reliably measuring the complexity of James' style. Such difficulties are probably inherent in the
counting of any stylistic feature, at least to some extent, and thus I
have not avoided a certain amount of arbitrary judgment by restricting
myself to the classification of nouns and verbs. For this analysis I ran
into more difficulties than in my analysis of *The Wings of the Dove*
because the letters and notebooks contain a much wider range of
grammatical forms, especially commands, appositives, and fragments.
To sort out the various features I used the following rules.

1. I counted each member of a compound subject as a separate
   subject, and each member of a compound verb as a separate
   verb.
2. I counted the deleted subjects of commands as active agents.
3. I counted the main noun in a fragment as a subject if it seemed
   to be a subject with a deleted predicate; I did not count it if it
   seemed to be an object. In the following example from the
   notebooks I counted *spell* and *charm* as subjects because they
   seemed parallel to *something,* the subject of the previous
   sentence: "(Oh, the kind little, sweet little spell, the charm, that
   still lurks in that phrase and process—small, sacred relic of
   those strange *scenario* days!)"
4. I counted appositives as subjects if it seemed appropriate. In
   the example above "the charm" seemed more like a compound
   than an appositive, so I counted it as a subject.
5. I counted indefinite pronouns and *one* as intangible nouns, not
   as active agents.

In order to determine whether the differences between James' private
and public styles were significant, I submitted the figures from table
2 in chapter 4 to a variety of statistical tests. I grouped both letter and
notebook samples together as private writing and determined their
combined average sentence length and the combined percentage of
each kind of noun and verb in each of the major categories. I did the
same for the figures for travel writing, criticism, and short story, group-
ing them together as published writing. I then conducted a median

Table 4
Features of James' Letters

				Addressee					
Feature	Mrs. de Navarro	S. Colvin	E. Gosse	H. Reubell	H. G. Wells	C. E. Norton	Total	Total %
Average Sentence Length								
No. of Sentences	5	32	9	31	23	30	130	
No. of Words	112	418	152	651	451	867	2,651	
Words/Sentence	22.4	13.06	16.89	21	19.6	28.9	20.4	
Nominals as Subjects of Main Clauses								
Active Agents	6	18	8	24	22	28	106	59.2
Tangible Nouns	2	2	0	5	0	1	10	5.6
Intangible Nouns (excluding deictics and expletives)	0	7	3	9	5	10	34	19
Deictic Pronouns	0	4	2	6	2	0	14	7.8
Expletives *it/there*	0	5	0	4	3	3	15	8.4
Combined Intangibles	0	16	5	19	10	13	63	35.2
Verbs of Main Clauses								
Stative	1	10	2	14	8	18	53	30.1
Active	7	24	11	32	22	24	120	68.2
Passive	0	0	0	0	1	2	3	1.7

Table 5
Features of James' Notebook

Feature		Oct 5.			Entry			
	1	2	3	4	Nov. 11	Nov. 12	Total	Total %
Average Sentence Length								
No. of Sentences	11	13	9	2	12	16	63	
No. of Words	211	268	232	32	386	319	1,448	
Words/Sentence	19.2	20.6	25.8	16	32.2	19.9	22.98	
Nominals as Subjects of Main Clauses								
Active Agents	4	8	5	1	4	14	36	50.7
Tangible Nouns	0	0	0	0	0	0	0	0
Intangible Nouns (excluding deictics and expletives)	7	4	1	0	5	4	21	29.6
Deictic Pronouns	1	1	1	0	3	2	8	11.3
Expletives *it/there*	1	1	0	0	2	2	6	8.5
Combined Intangibles	9	6	2	0	10	8	35	49.3
Verbs of Main Clauses (by page)	293–94		295		296–97			
Stative	5		1		9		15	21.4
Active	22		6		27		55	78.6
Passive	0		0		0		0	0

Table 6
Features of James' Travel Writing

Feature	Intro	Chapters				Total	Total %
		1	*2*	*3*	*4*		
Average Sentence Length							
No. of Sentences	5	18	16	36	18	93	
No. of Words	249	360	694	1,114	719	3,471	
Words/Sentence	49.8	20	43.4	30.9	39.9	37.3	
Nominals as Subjects of Main Clauses							
Active Agents	2	2	8	9	8	29	19.2
Tangible Nouns	1	1	0	10	10	22	14.6
Intangible Nouns (excluding deictics and expletives)	2	9	10	29	18	68	45
Deictic Pronouns	0	4	1	7	1	13	8.6
Expletives *it/there*	2	8	2	6	1	19	12.6
Combined Intangibles	5	21	13	42	20	100	66.2
Verbs of Main Clauses							
Stative	4	13	9	26	18	70	50
Active	3	9	11	27	11	61	43.6
Passive	0	1	1	3	4	9	6.4

Table 7
Features of James' Criticism

Feature	Pages				Total	Total %
	30–31	*32–33*	*34–35*	*36 (to end of 1st para.)*	*Total*	*Total %*
Average Sentence Length						
No. of Sentences	18	23	24	7	72	
No. of Words	582	714	774	259	2,329	
Words/Sentences	32.3	31.1	32.3	37	32.35	
Nominals as Subjects of Main Clauses						
Active Agents	0	3	3	1	7	7.2
Tangible Nouns	0	0	1	0	1	1
Intangible Nouns (excluding deictics and expletives)	16	12	18	4	50	51.5
Deictic Pronouns	7	11	5	4	27	27.8
Expletives *it/there*	2	3	6	1	12	12.4
Combined Intangibles	24	26	29	9	88	90.7
Verbs of Main Clauses						
Stative	13	14	18	5	50	49
Active	10	15	11	4	40	39.2
Passive	1	1	9	1	12	11.8

Table 8
Features of One of James' Stories

Feature	Pages					Total	Total %
	239	241	244–45	248	251–53		
Average Sentence Length							
No. of Sentences	3	6	14	8	28	59	
No. of Words	94	289	447	244	858	1,932	
Words/Sentences	31.3	48.2	31.9	30.5	30.6	32.75	
Nominals as Subjects of Main Clauses							
Active Agents	3	1	11	6	17	38	47.5
Tangible Nouns	0	0	2	0	2	4	5
Intangible Nouns (excluding deictics and expletives)	0	4	3	1	9	17	21.25
Deictic Pronouns	0	2	1	1	1	5	6.25
Expletives *it/there*	0	2	1	3	10	16	20
Combined Intangibles	0	8	5	5	20	38	47.5
Verbs of Main Clauses							
Stative	0	5	8	5	15	33	40.7
Active	3	3	10	6	22	44	54.3
Passive	0	1	0	0	3	4	4.9

Table 9
Statistical Tests of Difference Between James' Private and
Published Writing

Feature	Private	Published	Test Statistic (degrees of freedom)	Probability
Average Sentence Length				
Words/Sentence	21.2	34.5	$\chi^2 = 65.7$[a] $(df = 1)$	$p<.001$
Percentage of Nominals as Subjects of Main Clauses				
Active Agents	56.8	22.6	$\bar{z} = 8.419$[b]	$p<.001$
Tangible Nouns	4	8.2	$\bar{z} = 2.028$	$p<.05$
Combined Intangibles	39.2	69.2	$\bar{z} = 7.202$	$p<.001$
Percentage of Verbs in Main Clauses				
Stative	27.6	47.4	$\bar{z} = 4.783$	$p<.001$
Active	71.1	44.9	$\bar{z} = 6.194$	$p<.001$
Passive	1.2	7.7	$\chi^2 = 78.8$[c] $(df = 1)$	$p<.001$

Note: All statistical tests are from J. P. Guilford and Benjamin Fruchter, *Fundamental Statistics in Psychology and Education*, 5th ed. (New York: McGraw-Hill, 1973).

[a]Median test

[b]$\bar{z}$-test of significance for the difference between uncorrelated proportions

[c]χ^2 with Yates' correction for continuity

test on the differences between the combined average sentence length of the two groups and a $\bar{z}$-test of significance for the difference between the combined percentages of each kind of noun used as a subject and for the difference between the combined percentages of each kind of verb in the two groups. Because of the extremely small size of the sample of passive verbs, I had to use a χ^2 test of significance for the difference between the combined percentages of the passive in the two groups. The results are summarized in table 9. The differences were significant in all seven categories.

I might add that James' published work also exhibits considerable variety, enough variety so that the differences between the private and published writing are not obvious. The short story has more than twice as many active agents as subjects than the travel writing and almost nine times as many as the criticism (47.5 percent for the short story as opposed to 19.2 percent for the travel writing and 7.2 percent for the criticism). The criticism, on the other hand, has almost twice as many combined intangibles as subjects than the short story (90.7 percent as opposed to 47.5 percent). The travel writing, as we might expect from a description of places, has the most tangible nouns as subjects (14.6 percent as opposed to 1 percent in the criticism and 5 percent in the short story). The differences are less great for sentence length and the use of verbs, although the criticism does contain twice as many passives as the short story (11.8 percent as opposed to 4.9 percent). However we define James' published style, he did vary that style to meet the requirements of the topic and genre he was involved with at the time.

Notes

1. Introduction

1. William James, *The Letters of William James*, vol. 2, ed. Henry James [his son] (Boston: The Atlantic Monthly Press, 1920), p. 278. The letter is dated May 1907.

2. Roland Barthes, "Style and Its Image," in *Literary Style: A Symposium,* ed. Seymour Chatman (New York: Oxford Univ. Press, 1971), pp. 3-10. For two possible typologies of the various conventions or codes we use in interpreting literary works, see Roland Barthes, *S/Z*, trans. Richard Miller (New York: Hill and Wang, 1974), and Steven Mailloux, *Interpretive Conventions: The Reader in the Study of American Fiction* (Ithaca, NY: Cornell Univ. Press, 1982).

3. Richard Ohmann, "Generative Grammars and the Concept of Literary Style," in *Contemporary Essays on Style,* ed. Glen A. Love and Michael Payne (Glenview, IL: Scott, Foresman, 1969), p. 136.

2. Theories of Style

1. Laurence Holland, *The Expense of Vision: Essays on the Craft of Henry James* (Princeton: Princeton Univ. Press, 1964), pp. 87–88.

2. F. O. Matthiessen, *Henry James: The Major Phase* (New York: Oxford Univ. Press, 1944), pp. 155–59, passim.

3. Joseph Warren Beach, *The Method of Henry James* (Philadelphia: Albert Saifer, Publisher, 1954), pp. 111–12.

4. Austin Warren, *Rage for Order: Essays in Criticism* (Ann Arbor: The Univ. of Michigan Press, 1959), p. 143.

5. F. R. Leavis, *The Great Tradition* (New York: New York Univ. Press, 1967), p. 168.

6. Richard Ohmann, "Generative Grammars," pp. 146–47.

7. Roger Fowler, *Linguistics and the Novel* (London: Methuen and Company, Ltd., 1977), p. 111.

8. Geoffrey Leech and Michael Short, *Style in Fiction* (New York: Longman, 1981), pp. 97–110; 195–96.

9. See for example J. B. Goldenthal, "Henry James and Impressionism: A

Method of Stylistic Analysis," Diss. New York University, 1974; Leo T. Hendrick, "Henry James: The Late and Early Styles," Diss. University of Michigan, 1953; Robert G. Johnson, "A Study of the Style of Henry James's Late Novels," Diss. Bowling Green State University, 1971; William F. Smith, Jr., "Sentence Structure in the Tales of Henry James," *Style* 7 (1973): 157–72; Bruce Philip Tracy, "Henry James's Representation of Inner Consciousness in Meditation Scenes from the Late Novels," Diss. Michigan State University, 1971; L. S. Wilson, "The Stylistics of Henry James: A Linguistic Analysis of Selected Early and Late Novels," Diss. Florida State University, 1974.

10. Seymour Chatman, *The Later Style of Henry James* (Oxford: Basil Blackwell, 1972), pp. 6–7.

11. I leave for later a discussion of the best attempts to bridge the gap between detailed linguistic analysis and critical judgment—Ian Watt's essay on the first paragraph of *The Ambassadors* and David Lodge's chapter on that same novel in his book *Language of Fiction.*

12. F. R. Leavis in *The Importance of Scrutiny,* ed. Eric Bentley (New York: Grove Press, 1957), pp. 31–32. Wellek's letter-review is on pp. 23–30. Leavis' reply is on pp. 30–40.

13. See for example René Wellek, "Closing Statement," in *Style in Language,* ed. Thomas Sebeok (Cambridge, MA: The MIT Press, 1960), pp. 408–19; and René Wellek, "Stylistics, Poetics, and Criticism," in *Literary Style: A Symposium,* ed. Seymour Chatman (New York: Oxford Univ. Press, 1971), pp. 65–75, especially p. 68.

14. Roger Fowler, *Literature as Social Discourse* (Bloomington: Indiana Univ. Press, 1981), pp. 19, 22.

15. Stanley Fish, *Is There a Text in This Class?* (Cambridge, MA: Harvard Univ. Press, 1980). See especially the chapters "What Is Stylistics and Why Are They Saying Such Terrible Things About It?" Pts. 1 and 2, pp. 68–96 and 246–67. Also Barbara Herrnstein Smith, *On the Margins of Discourse: The Relation of Literature to Language* (Chicago: The Univ. of Chicago Press, 1978). See pt.7: "Surfacing from the Deep," pp. 157–201.

The first major response to Fowler was by F. W. Bateson. Their exchange is recorded in *Essays in Criticism* 17 (1967):322–47; and 18 (1968):164–82. It is reprinted in Roger Fowler, *The Languages of Literature* (New York: Barnes and Noble, 1971), pp. 43–79.

16. Fowler, *Literature as Social Discourse,* p. 178. Fowler's proposal, however, does not answer the objections of Fish and Smith. For his comments on them see pp. 174–77.

17. William F. Smith, Jr., pp. 157–72.

18. Barry Menikoff, "Punctuation and Point of View in the Late Style of Henry James," *Style* 4 (1970): 29.

19. Ludwig Wittgenstein, *Philosophical Investigations,* 2d ed., trans. G. E. M. Anscombe (New York: Macmillan, 1968). See especially secs. 66 and 67.

20. For a rigorous defense of New Criticism, see Murray Krieger, *The New Apologists for Poetry* (Bloomington: Indiana Univ. Press, 1963).

21. Louise Rosenblatt, *Literature as Exploration* (New York: Appleton-Century, 1938). A more recent edition was published by the Modern Language Association in 1983.

22. See Roman Ingarden, *The Literary Work of Art,* trans. by George G.

Grabowicz (Evanston, IL: Northwestern Univ. Press, 1973) and his *Cognition of the Literary Work of Art,* trans. Ruth Ann Crowley and Kenneth R. Olson (Evanston, IL: Northwestern Univ. Press, 1973), as well as Wolfgang Iser, *The Act of Reading: A Theory of Aesthetic Response* (Baltimore: The Johns Hopkins Univ. Press, 1978).

23. Norman Holland, *5 Readers Reading* (New Haven: Yale Univ. Press, 1975), and David Bleich, *Subjective Criticism* (Baltimore: The Johns Hopkins Univ. Press, 1978).

24. See especially pt. 2 of *Is There a Text in This Class?* pp. 303–71. For a fine summary of the debate about where meaning resides in the reading process, see Michael Steig, "Reading and Meaning," *College English* 44 (1982):182–89. Steig identifies the underlying issue in pedagogy as one of power: who is going to decide what a literary work means?

25. René Wellek and Austin Warren, *Theory of Literature,* 3d ed. (New York: Harcourt, 1956). See "The Mode of Existence of a Literary Work of Art," pp. 142–57.

26. For an argument in favor of dualism, see Louis Milic, "Theories of Style and Their Implications for the Teaching of Composition," in *Contemporary Essays on Style,* ed. Glen A. Love and Michael Payne (Glenview, IL: Scott, Foresman, 1969), pp. 15–21.

27. Benedetto Croce, *Aesthetics,* trans. Douglas Ainshe (London: Macmillan, 1909). Much of the problem results from the way Croce uses terms to encompass very broad concepts, but he does clearly assert the identity of intuition, impression, and expression. The key chaps. are 1, 2, and 15.

28. Wayne C. Booth, *The Rhetoric of Fiction* (Chicago: The Univ. of Chicago Press, 1961), p. 313.

29. Many aesthetic monists will not grant, however, that what they mean by *meaning* is effect. See W. K. Wimsatt, "The Affective Fallacy," in *The Verbal Icon* (Lexington: Univ. of Kentucky Press, 1954), pp. 21–39. This essay was written with Monroe C. Beardsley.

30. Ian Watt, "The First Paragraph of *The Ambassadors:* An Explication," in *Contemporary Essays on Style,* ed. Glen A. Love and Michael Payne (Glenview, IL: Scott, Foresman, 1969), p. 276.

31. Sidney J. Krause, "James's Revisions of the Style of *The Portrait of a Lady,*" *American Literature* 30 (1958):78.

32. William James, *The Principles of Psychology,* vol. 1 (New York: Dover Publications, 1950). See especially the chapters on the stream of thought (9) and attention (11). For a survey of the research on mental process, see Dan Slobin, *Psycholinguistics* (Glenview, IL: Scott, Foresman, 1971), pp. 100–133.

33. James Britton, "Shaping at the Point of Utterance," in *Reinventing the Rhetorical Tradition,* eds. Aviva Freedman and Ian Pringle (Conway, AR: L & S Books, 1980), pp. 61–65.

34. For a brief survey of schema theory, see David Rumelhart, "Schemata: The Building Blocks of Cognition," in *Comprehension and Teaching: Research Reviews,* ed. John T. Guthrie (Newark, NJ: International Reading Association, 1981), pp. 3–26. See also Richard C. Anderson, "The Notion of Schemata and the Educational Enterprise," in *Schooling and the Acquisition of Knowledge,* eds. Richard C. Anderson, Rand Spiro, and William Montague (Hillsdale, NJ: Erlbaum, 1977), pp. 415–31.

35. Marcel Adam Just and Patricia A. Carpenter, "A Theory of Reading: From Eye Fixations to Comprehension," *Psychological Review* 87 (1980):331.

36. Louise Rosenblatt, "Transaction Versus Interaction—A Terminological Rescue Operation," *Research in the Teaching of English* 19 (1985):96–107. For an explanation of the difference between efferent and aesthetic reading, see chap. 3 of *The Reader, The Text, The Poem* (Carbondale: Southern Illinois Univ. Press, 1978), pp. 22–47.

37. Eliseo Vivas, *Creation and Discovery* (Chicago: Henry Regnery, 1955), p. 146.

38. See for example the work by Eugene Kintgen on how individual readers attack the reading of poems: "Studying the Perception of Poetry," in *Researching Response to Literature and the Teaching of Literature*, ed. Charles Cooper (Norwood, NJ: Ablex, 1985), pp. 128–50.

39. Jacques Barzun, *A Stroll with William James* (New York: Harper and Row, 1983), p. 71.

40. Fowler, *Linguistics and the Novel*, p. 109.

41. Ibid., p. 113.

42. Ibid., p. 111.

43. I am, of course, indebted to Stanley Fish for this argument. See especially his first essay on stylistics in *Is There a Text in This Class?* pp. 68–96.

44. The notion that stylistic analyses are, in some sense, circular has a long history. Its most famous expression is in Leo Spitzer's idea of "the philological circle," but Spitzer claimed to be explicating "the mind of the author." See *Linguistics and Literary History: Essays in Stylistics* (Princeton: Princeton Univ. Press, 1948), especially the title essay on pp. 1–39.

45. Both Gerald Graff and Kathleen McCormick have pointed out that Fish's latest position asserting the determining nature of interpretive communities does not account for individual differences within a community or for the ability of an individual reader-critic to suddenly realize a new perspective. See Graff, "Interpretation on Tlön: A Response to Stanley Fish," *New Literary History* 17 (1985):109–17, and McCormick, "Swimming Upstream with Stanley Fish," *The Journal of Aesthetics and Art Criticism* 44 (1985):67–76.

46. See Holland, *5 Readers*, and Bleich, *Subjective Criticism*. For a response similar to my own view, see Jane P. Tompkins, "Criticism and Feeling," *College English* 39 (1977):169–78. Tompkins argues that much reader-response criticism makes our responses the subject of criticism rather than the text. Holland and Bleich have admitted as much. See Norman Holland, "Unity Identity Text Self," *PMLA* 90 (1975):815, and David Bleich, "The Subjective Character of Critical Interpretation," *College English* 36 (1975):754.

47. See Jane P. Tompkins, "The Reader in History: The Changing Shape of Literary Response," in *Reader-Response Criticism*, ed. Jane P. Tompkins (Baltimore: The Johns Hopkins Univ. Press, 1980), pp. 201–32.

48. George Dillon, *Language Processing and the Reading of Literature* (Bloomington: Indiana Univ. Press, 1978), pp. xvii–xx, passim.

49. For an explication of the philosophical problems involved in constructing a model of literary reading that incorporates the concepts of "concretization" and the critical analysis of that "concretization," see William Ray, *Literary Meaning* (Oxford: Basil Blackwell, 1984), especially pp. 41–56 on Ingarden and Iser.

50. Fowler, *Literature as Social Discourse*, p. 66.

51. Talbot J. Taylor, *Linguistic Theory and Structural Stylistics* (New York: Pergamon Press, 1980).

52. For an explanation of how we establish a text from the perspective of reader-response criticism, see Steven Mailloux, especially chap. 4: "Textual Scholarship and 'Author's Final Intentions,' " pp. 93–125. In addition, George Dillon has demonstrated how our selective attention determines something as simple as a plot, a point he uses to refute Iser's comment that we often agree on the plot. See "Styles of Reading," *Poetics Today* 3 (1982):77–88.

53. For a sample of the wide variety of possible readings for "The Turn of the Screw," see "Essays in Criticism" in Henry James, *The Turn of the Screw,* ed. Robert Kimbrough (New York: W. W. Norton, 1966), pp. 169–273.

54. Thomas Bever, "A Cognitive Basis for Linguistic Structures," in *Cognition and the Development of Language,* ed. John R. Hayes (New York: Wiley, 1970), p. 297.

55. David Lodge, *Language of Fiction* (New York: Columbia Univ. Press, 1966), p. 207.

56. For a defense of introspective accounts of mental processes and their reliability, see K. Anders Ericsson and Herbert A. Simon, "Verbal Reports as Data," *Psychological Review* 87 (1980): 215–51. For an application of their ideas to the study of writing processes, see Barbara Tomlinson, "Talking About the Composing Process: The Limitations of Retrospective Accounts," *Written Communication* 1 (1984):429–45.

57. See Richard E. Nisbett and Timothy Wilson, "Telling More than We Can Know: Verbal Reports as Data," *Psychological Review* 84 (1977):231–59; and Timothy Wilson, Jay Hull, and Jim Johnson, "Awareness and Self-Perception: Verbal Reports on Internal States," *Journal of Personality and Social Psychology* 40 (1981): 53–71. For a summary of the arguments against the reliability of introspection, see Steven P. Stich, *From Folk Psychology to Cognitive Science* (Cambridge, MA; The MIT Press, 1983), pp. 228–42.

58. George Mandler has argued that consciousness itself needs to be accounted for by codes, rules, and conventions. See his *Cognitive Psychology: An Essay in Cognitive Science* (Hillsdale, NJ: Erlbaum, 1985), pp. 63–65.

59. Vernon Lee, *The Handling of Words and Other Studies in Literary Psychology* (New York: Dodd, Mead, 1923), p. 244.

60. Chatman, *Later Style of Henry James,* p. 58.

61. Mary Cross, "Henry James and the Grammar of the Modern," *The Henry James Review* 3 (1981):36, 40. In a later article Cross makes the metaphoric nature of her claims clearer. She talks about "the system of meaning" which the sentences of *The Ambassadors* "perform," Strether's "process of seeing, which the repetitive pattern of parallelism accommodates and enacts," and James's syntax becoming metaphor. See "The 'Drama of Discrimination': Style as Plot in *The Ambassadors,*" *Language and Style* 18 (1985):47, 51, 55.

62. William Veeder, *Henry James—The Lessons of the Master* (Chicago: The Univ. of Chicago Press, 1975), p. 214.

63. Dillon, *Language Processing,* pp. xxvii-xxviii.

64. Indeed, William Ray argues that we cannot know the conventions involved in a particular interpretation while we are engaged in that interpretation. To do so we must step outside our interpretation and apply a new set of

conventions, thus leading to an infinite regress of convention and interpretation. George Mandler applies the same argument to consciousness: to understand consciousness we must posit some forms of mental structure, but these structures in turn must be understood in terms of still more structures. A philosophical defense of codes, rules, and conventions would take me far afield. Ray points out three ways of handling the problem of infinite regress: total relativism, belief, and submersion in the rhetorical process. For the sake of the ongoing practice of criticism, I would champion both belief and relativism in constant tension—as Ray does.

3. *Style as Identification*

1. Benjamin Franklin, quoted in Carl Klaus, "Reflections on Prose Style," in *Contemporary Essays on Style,* ed. Glen A. Love and Michael Payne (Glenview, IL: Scott, Foresman, 1969), p. 56.

2. Klaus, pp. 57, 59.

3. George Dillon, *Language Processing,* p. 160.

4. Seymour Chatman, *Later Style of Henry James,* p. 72.

5. Hendrick, pp. 129-32.

6. The rationale for Chatman's study is the desire to identify the most effective parody of James' late work.

7. Tracy, p. 84.

8. Bennison Gray, *Style: The Problem and Its Solution* (The Hague: Mouton, 1969). See especially chap. 5, pp. 66-73.

9. Gary Sloan, "Mistaking Subject Matter for Style," *College English* 43 (1981):502-7.

10. Max Beerbohm, as quoted in Chatman, *Later Style of Henry James,* p. 114.

11. Another famous example is the utilitarian product which the Newsomes manufacture in *The Ambassadors* but which James never specifies.

12. Charles R. Crow, "The Style of Henry James: *The Wings of the Dove,*" in *Style in Prose Fiction: English Institute Essays, 1958,* ed. Harold C. Martin (New York: Columbia Univ. Press, 1959), p. 173.

13. David Lodge quotes a passage of about eight hundred words from the recognition scene in *The Ambassadors,* but he closely analyzes only a small part of the entire passage—about half of it. See Lodge, pp. 198–213.

14. Crow, p. 173.

15. Chatman, *Later Style of Henry James,* pp. 9–10; Dorothea Krook, "The Method of the Later Works of Henry James," *London Magazine* 1 (1954):55–58; Lee, pp. 245–46.

16. Hendrick, p. 3; William F. Smith, Jr., p. 163.

17. Leech and Short, p. 228.

18. Chatman, *Later Style of Henry James,* p. 100.

4. *Style as Expression*

1. Darshan Singh Maini, *Henry James: The Indirect Vision* (Bombay: Tata McGraw-Hill Publishing Company, Ltd., 1973), p. 186.

2. R. W. Short, "The Sentence Structure of Henry James," *American Literature* 18 (1946):88.

3. Jane B. Tompkins, "'The Beast in the Jungle': An Analysis of James's Late Style," *Modern Fiction Studies* 16 (1970):188.

4. Chatman, *Later Style of Henry James*, p. 100.

5. Leech and Short, p. 228.

6. Alan Tormey, *The Concept of Expression: A Study in Philosophical Psychology and Aesthetics* (Princeton: Princeton Univ. Press, 1971), p. 141.

7. Frank Sibley, "Aesthetic Concepts," in *Art and Philosophy*, ed. W. E. Kennick (New York: St. Martin's, 1964), p. 351.

8. Ibid., p. 355.

9. Ibid., p. 353.

10. W. E. Kennick, "Expression, Creativity, Truth, and Form," in *Art and Philosophy*, ed. W. E. Kennick (New York: St. Martin's, 1964), p. 382.

11. Richard Ohmann, "Mentalism in the Study of Literary Language," in *Proceedings of the Conference on Language and Language Behavior*, ed. Eric M. Zale (New York: Appleton-Century-Crofts, 1968), p. 200.

12. Ibid., p. 202.

13. Ibid.

14. Maini, pp. 186–99, passim.

15. John Halverson, "Late Manner, Major Phase," *Sewanee Review* 79 (1971):228.

16. Ibid., pp. 227–29.

17. Ibid., p. 222.

18. Richard Hocks, *Henry James and Pragmatistic Thought* (Chapel Hill: The Univ. of North Carolina Press, 1974), p. 4.

19. Ibid., p. 46.

20. Ibid., p. 54.

21. Henry James, quoted in ibid., p. 52.

22. Hocks, p. 79.

23. Leon Edel, *Henry James: The Treacherous Years 1895–1901* (New York: Avon Books, 1969), p. 317.

24. Theodora Bosanquet, *Henry James at Work* (London: The Hogarth Essays, n.d.), p. 247.

25. Ibid., p. 248.

26. Ibid., p. 247.

27. I have not been able to determine authoritatively whether the first five letters I have examined were handwritten or dictated. According to Leon Edel's edition of James' letters, the one on November 24 to Charles Eliot Norton was dictated. See *Henry James: Letters*, vol. 4, ed. Leon Edel (Cambridge, MA: Belknap Press, 1984), p. 120. Certainly by my analysis, the letter to Norton differs from the others in two ways: it has substantially longer sentences and a much higher proportion of stative verbs in main clauses, which would indicate that it may have been composed in a different way than the other letters. On the other hand, the subjects of the sentences are of substantially the same kind in all five letters. (See app. B, table 4.) My main point, however, is that whether he was writing by hand or dictating, James seems to have had a different style in his private writing than he had in his published work.

28. Arthur Benson, quoted in Simon Nowell-Smith, ed., *The Legend of the Master* (New York: Scribner's, 1948), pp. 138–39.

29. Nowell-Smith, and Norman Page, *Henry James: Interviews and Recollections* (London: Macmillan, 1984).

30. Page, pp. xiv–xv.

31. Quoted in Page, p. 75. There are a few examples of James' speech which approximate the public style. See for example James Whitall's recollection in Nowell-Smith, p. 107, and Arthur Benson's in Page, p. 112. Since these are the exceptions we must wonder how much these men heard what they wanted to hear.

32. Henry James, quoted in F. O. Matthiessen, ed., *The James Family* (New York: Vintage Books, 1980), p. 338.

33. Henry James, *The Notebooks of Henry James*, ed. F. O. Matthiessen and Kenneth B. Murdock (New York: Oxford Univ. Press, 1961), p. 179.

34. Henry James, *Notes of a Son and Brother* (London: Macmillan, 1914); Leon Edel, *Henry James: The Untried Years 1843–1870* (New York: Avon Books, 1953), p. 236; William James, *Letters*, p. 288.

35. For reconstructions of James' speech in the days before tape recorders, see Nowell-Smith, especially pp. 16–17, 107, 114–15, and 141; and Page, especially pp. 75 and 107.

36. H. G. Wells, quoted in *Henry James and H. G. Wells*, ed. Leon Edel and Gordon N. Ray (Urbana: Univ. of Illinois Press, 1958), pp. 245–48.

37. Henry James, quoted in Edel and Ray, p. 267.

5. *Style as Imitation*

1. Crow, pp. 175–76.

2. Chatman, *Later Style of Henry James*, p. 104.

3. Hisayoshi Watanabe, "Past Perfect Retrospection in the Style of Henry James," *American Literature* 34 (1962):175.

4. Tompkins, "Beast in the Jungle," p. 190.

5. Fish, pp. 247–51; Barbara Herrnstein Smith, pp. 158–62.

6. Barbara Herrnstein Smith, pp. 160–61.

7. Ibid., p. 161.

8. Winston Weathers, "The Rhetoric of the Series," in *Contemporary Essays on Style*, ed. Glen A. Love and Michael Payne (Glenview, IL: Scott, Foresman, 1969), pp. 21–27; Richard Weaver, "Some Rhetorical Aspects of Grammatical Categories," in *The Ethics of Rhetoric* (Chicago: Henry Regnery, 1953), pp. 115–42; Louis Ceci, "The Case for Syntactic Imagery," *College English* 45 (1983):431–49.

9. Smith, p. 152.

10. Ibid., pp. 152–53.

11. Quoted in George Dillon, *Language Processing*, pp. 175–76.

12. Ibid., p. 176.

13. Watt, pp. 266–83; Percy Lubbock, *The Craft of Fiction* (New York: Viking Press, 1957), pp. 156–71; Tompkins, "Beast in the Jungle," pp. 185–91; Gordon O. Taylor, *The Passages of Thought: Psychological Representation in the American Novel 1870–1900* (New York: Oxford Univ. Press, 1969).

14. Veeder, p. 66.
15. Gordon O. Taylor, pp. 5–6.
16. William James, *Principles,* p. 225. It is, perhaps, an indication of the difficulty in using Henry's prose as a metaphor for William's conception of mental life that William did not see the connection himself. As far as I know, William never comments that Henry has managed to capture in his style some aspect of the stream of consciousness.
17. Veeder, pp. 210–11.
18. Leech and Short, p. 337. For another typology see Dorrit Cohn, *Transparent Minds: Narrative Modes of Presenting Consciousness in Fiction* (Princeton: Princeton Univ. Press, 1978). Cohn includes both Narrative Report and Indirect Thought under what he calls "Psycho-narration"; he terms Direct Thought "Quoted Monologue" and he calls Free Indirect Thought "Narrated Monologue."
19. For a defense of various modes of presenting thought before the "stream of consciousness" technique, see Cohn, pp. 11–14.
20. For a critical history of Free Indirect Discourse in English and American literature, see Roy Pascal, *The Dual Voice* (Manchester: Manchester Univ. Press, 1977), pp. 34–141.
21. Ibid., p. 137.
22. George Eliot, quoted in ibid., pp. 82–83.
23. For the most complete summary of Free Indirect Discourse and the issues involved in describing the form linguistically, see Brian McHale, "Free Indirect Discourse: A Survey of Recent Accounts," *PTL: A Journal for Descriptive Poetics and Theory of Literature* 3 (1978):249–87. McHale argues convincingly that there are no purely formal cues for determining FID, that semantics is the only reliable indicator.
24. Franz Stanzel, *Narrative Situations in the Novel,* trans. James P. Pusack (Bloomington: Indiana Univ. Press, 1971).
25. A similar point is made by Seymour Chatman in "The Structure of Narrative Transmissions," in *Style and Structure in Literature: Essays in the New Stylistics,* ed. Roger Fowler (Ithaca, NY: Cornell Univ. Press, 1975), pp. 213–57.
26. Edel, *Untried Years,* p. 218.
27. Paul Hernadi, "Free Indirect Discourse and Related Techniques," in *Beyond Genre: New Directions in Literary Classification* (Ithaca, NY: Cornell Univ. Press, 1972), p. 196.
28. Henry James, *The Portrait of a Lady,* ed. Robert Bamberg (New York: Norton, 1975). All further references are to this edition, which uses the 1908 text. I have checked Bamberg's list of changes between this edition and the earlier one of 1881 to be sure there are no substantial differences in the passages I use. For Bamberg's Textual Notes, see pp. 493–575.
29. Cohn, pp. 129–30.
30. But see Banfield on the danger of using a shift to the first person as a test for Free Indirect Discourse, pp. 23–63. In Banfield's theory FID has an entirely different transformational history than direct discourse and therefore it cannot be translated into the more explicit form. Banfield's argument hinges on the concept of narratorless sentences, by which she means sentences that can express a point of view without indicating a speaker. According to Banfield,

if a speaker is not indicated by grammatical cues, a sentence cannot by definition express the point of view of a specific person. Thus direct discourse has both a marked speaker and point of view, while FID has no marked speaker, which means those sentences cannot indicate the point of view of the narrator.

31. Stanzel, especially pp. 99–120, his discussion of *The Ambassadors.*

32. Chatman, *Later Styles of Henry James,* pp. 10–22; Michael Shriber, "Cognitive Apparatus in *Daisy Miller, The Ambassadors,* and Two Works by Howells: A Comparative Study of the Epistemology of Henry James," *Language and Style* 2 (1969):207–25.

33. Lodge, p. 204.

6. Conclusion: The Limits of Stylistic Criticism

1. Watt, p. 275.

2. Ibid., p. 274.

3. Ibid., p. 275.

4. Ibid., pp. 271–272.

5. Ibid., pp. 273–274, passim.

6. Ibid., p. 276.

7. Ibid., pp. 273–274.

8. Ibid., p. 280.

9. Kathleen McCormick, "Psychological Realism: A New Epistemology for Reader-Response Criticism," *Reader,* no. 14 (1985):46.

10. The words of Josephine Miles may apply to James: "Style is what it is; what it is has deep involvement with what, linguistically, artistically, evaluatively, individually, it is not." See "Style as Style," in *Literary Style: A Symposium,* ed. Seymour Chatman (New York: Oxford Univ. Press, 1971), p. 28.

11. See my analysis of the periodic structures in "The Beast in the Jungle": "The Leap of the Beast: The Dramatic Style of Henry James's 'The Beast in the Jungle,' " *The Henry James Review* 4 (1983):219–30.

Bibliography

Anderson, Richard C. "The Notion of Schemata and the Educational Enterprise."
In *Schooling and the Acquisition of Knowledge.* Ed. Richard C. Anderson,
Rand Spiro, and William Montague. Hillsdale, NJ: Erlbaum, 1977.

Banfield, Ann. *Unspeakable Sentences: Narration and Representation in the
Language of Fiction.* Boston: Routledge and Kegan Paul, 1982.

Barthes, Roland. "Style and Its Image." In *Literary Style: A Symposium.* Ed.
Seymour Chatman. New York: Oxford Univ. Press, 1971.

————. *S/Z.* Trans. Richard Miller. New York: Hill and Wang, 1974.

Barzun, Jacques. *A Stroll With William James.* New York: Harper and Row,
1983.

Beach, Joseph Warren. *The Method of Henry James.* Philadelphia: Albert Saifer,
Publisher, 1954.

Bentley, Eric, ed. *The Importance of Scrutiny.* New York: Grove Press, 1957.

Bever, Thomas. "A Cognitive Basis for Linguistic Structures." In *Cognition and
the Development of Language.* Ed. John R. Hayes. New York: Wiley,
1970.

Bleich, David. "The Subjective Character of Critical Interpretation." *College
English* 36 (1975):739–55.

————. *Subjective Criticism.* Baltimore: The Johns Hopkins Univ. Press, 1978.

Booth, Wayne C. *The Rhetoric of Fiction.* Chicago: The Univ. of Chicago Press,
1961.

Bosanquet, Theodora. *Henry James at Work.* London: The Hogarth Essays, n.d.

Britton, James. "Shaping at the Point of Utterance." In *Reinventing the Rhetorical Tradition.* Ed. Aviva Freedman and Ian Pringle. Conway, AR: L &
S Books, 1980.

Ceci, Louis. "The Case for Syntactic Imagery." *College English* 45 (1983):431–
49.

Chatman, Seymour. *The Later Style of Henry James.* Oxford: Basil Blackwell,
1972.

————, ed. *Literary Style: A Symposium.* New York: Oxford Univ. Press, 1971.

————. "The Structure of Narrative Transmissions." In *Style and Structure in
Literature: Essays in the New Stylistics.* Ed. Roger Fowler. Ithaca, NY:
Cornell Univ. Press, 1975.

Cohn, Dorrit. *Transparent Minds: Narrative Modes of Presenting Consciousness in Fiction.* Princeton: Princeton Univ. Press, 1978.

Croce, Benedetto. *Aesthetics.* Trans. Douglas Ainshe. London: Macmillan, 1909.

Cross, Mary. "The 'Drama of Discrimination': Style as Plot in *The Ambassadors.*" *Language and Style* 18 (1985):46–63.

———. "Henry James and the Grammar of the Modern." *The Henry James Review* 3 (1981):33–43.

Crow, Charles R. "The Style of Henry James: *The Wings of the Dove.*" In *Style in Prose Fiction: English Institute Essays, 1958.* Ed. Harold C. Martin. New York: Columbia Univ. Press, 1959.

Culler, Jonathan. *Structuralist Poetics.* Ithaca, NY: Cornell Univ. Press, 1975.

Dillon, George. *Language Processing and the Reading of Literature.* Bloomington: Indiana Univ. Press, 1978.

———. "Styles of Reading." *Poetics Today* 3 (1982):77–88.

Edel, Leon. *Henry James: The Conquest of London 1870–1881.* New York: Avon Books, 1962.

———. *Henry James: The Master 1901–1916.* New York: Avon Books, 1972.

———. *Henry James: The Middle Years 1882–1895.* New York: Avon Books, 1962.

———. *Henry James: The Treacherous Years 1895–1901.* New York: Avon Books, 1969.

———. *Henry James: The Untried Years 1843–1870.* New York: Avon Books, 1953.

———, and Gordon N. Ray, eds. *Henry James and H. G. Wells.* Urbana: Univ. of Illinois Press, 1958.

Ericsson, K. Anders, and Herbert A. Simon. "Verbal Reports as Data." *Psychological Review* 87 (1980):215–51.

Fish, Stanley. *Is There a Text in This Class?* Cambridge, MA: Harvard Univ. Press, 1980.

Fowler, Roger. *The Languages of Literature.* New York: Barnes and Noble, 1971.

———. *Linguistics and the Novel.* London: Methuen and Company, Ltd., 1977.

———. *Literature as Social Discourse.* Bloomington: Indiana Univ. Press, 1981.

———, ed. *Style and Structure in Literature: Essays in the New Stylistics.* Ithaca, NY: Cornell Univ. Press, 1975.

Gale, Robert. *The Caught Image: Figurative Language in the Fiction of Henry James.* Chapel Hill: The Univ. of North Carolina Press, 1964.

Goldenthal, J. B. "Henry James and Impressionism: A Method of Stylistic Analysis." Diss. New York University, 1974.

Graff, Gerald. "Interpretation on Tlön: A Response to Stanley Fish." *New Literary History* 17 (1985):109–17.

Gray, Bennison. *Style: The Problem and Its Solution.* The Hague: Mouton, 1969.

Halverson, John. "Late Manner, Major Phase." *Sewanee Review* 79 (1971):214–31.

Hendrick, Leo T. "Henry James: The Late and Early Styles." Diss. University of Michigan, 1953.

Hernadi, Paul. *Beyond Genre: New Directions in Literary Classification.* Ithaca, NY: Cornell Univ. Press, 1972.

Hocks, Richard. *Henry James and Pragmatistic Thought.* Chapel Hill: The Univ. of North Carolina Press, 1974.

Holland, Laurence. *The Expense of Vision: Essays on the Craft of Henry James.* Princeton: Princeton Univ. Press, 1964.

Holland, Norman. *5 Readers Reading.* New Haven: Yale Univ. Press, 1975.

———. "Unity Identity Text Self." *PLMA* 90 (1975): 813–22.

Ingarden, Roman. *The Cognition of the Literary Work of Art.* Trans. Ruth Ann Crowley and Kenneth R. Olson. Evanston, IL: Northwestern Univ. Press, 1973.

———. *The Literary Work of Art.* Trans. George G. Grabowicz. Evanston, IL: Northwestern Univ. Press, 1975.

Iser, Wolfgang. *The Art of Reading: A Theory of Aesthetic Response.* Baltimore: The Johns Hopkins Univ. Press, 1978.

James, Henry. *The Complete Tales.* 12 vols. Ed. Leon Edel. London: Rupert Hart-Davis, 1962–64.

———. *The Future of the Novel.* Ed. Leon Edel. New York: Vintage Books, 1956.

———. *Henry James: Letters.* Vol. 4. Ed. Leon Edel. Cambridge, MA: Belknap Press, 1984.

———. *Italian Hours.* New York: Grove Press, n.d.

———. *The Letters of Henry James.* Vol. 1. Ed. Percy Lubbock. New York: Octagon Books, 1970.

———. *The Notebooks of Henry James.* Ed. F. O. Matthiessen and Kenneth B. Murdock. New York: Oxford Univ. Press, 1961.

———. *Notes of a Son and Brother.* London: Macmillan, 1914.

———. *The Novels and Tales.* 26 vols. New York: Scribner's, 1907–9.

———. *The Portrait of a Lady.* Ed. Robert Bamberg. New York: Norton, 1975.

———. *The Sacred Fount.* New York: Grove Press, 1953.

———. *The Turn of the Screw.* Ed. Robert Kimbrough. New York: Norton, 1966.

James, William. *The Letters of William James.* Vol. 2. Ed. Henry James [his son]. Boston: The Atlantic Monthly Press, 1920.

———. *The Principles of Psychology.* Vol. 1. New York: Dover Publications, 1950.

Johnson, Robert G. "A Study of the Style of Henry James' Late Novels." Diss. Bowling Green State University, 1971.

Just, Marcel Adam, and Patricia A. Carpenter. "A Theory of Reading: From Eye Fixations to Comprehension." *Psychological Review* 87 (1980):329–54.

Kennick, W. E. "Expression, Creativity, Truth, and Form." In *Art and Philosophy.* Ed. W. E. Kennick. New York: St. Martin's, 1964.

Kintgen, Eugene. "Studying the Perception of Poetry." In *Researching Response to Literature and the Teaching of Literature.* Ed. Charles Cooper. Norwood, NJ: Ablex, 1985.

Klaus, Carl. "Reflections on Prose Style." In *Contemporary Essays on Style.* Ed. Glen A. Love and Michael Payne. Glenview, IL: Scott, Foresman, 1969.

Krause, Sydney J. "James's Revisions of the Style of *The Portrait of a Lady.*" *American Literature* 30 (1958):67–88.

Krieger, Murray. *The New Apologists for Poetry.* Bloomington: Indiana Univ. Press, 1963.

Krook, Dorothea. "The Method of the Later Works of Henry James." *London Magazine* 1 (1954):55–70.

———. *The Ordeal of Consciousness in Henry James.* Cambridge: Cambridge Univ. Press, 1962.

Leavis. F. R. *The Great Tradition.* New York: New York Univ. Press, 1967.

Lee, Vernon [Violet Piaget]. *The Handling of Words and Other Studies in Literary Psychology.* New York: Dodd, Mead, 1923.

Leech, Geoffrey, and Michael Short. *Style in Fiction.* New York: Longman, 1981.

Lodge, David. *Language of Fiction.* New York: Columbia Univ. Press, 1966.

Lubbock, Percy. *The Craft of Fiction.* New York: Viking, 1957.

McCormick, Kathleen. "Psychological Realism: A New Epistemology for Reader-Response Criticism." *Reader,* no. 14 (1985):40–53.

———. "Swimming Upstream with Stanley Fish." *The Journal of Aesthetics and Art Criticism* 44 (1985):67–76.

McHale, Brian. "Free Indirect Discourse: A Survey of Recent Accounts." *PTL: A Journal for Descriptive Poetics and Theory of Literature* 3 (1978):249–87.

Mailloux, Steven. *Interpretive Conventions: The Reader in the Study of American Fiction.* Ithaca, NY: Cornell Univ. Press, 1982.

Maini, Darshan Singh. *Henry James: The Indirect Vision.* Bombay: Tata McGraw-Hill Publishing Company, Ltd., 1973.

Mandler, George. *Cognitive Psychology: An Essay in Cognitive Science.* Hillsdale, NJ: Erlbaum, 1985.

Matthiessen, F. O. *Henry James: The Major Phase.* New York: Oxford Univ. Press, 1944.

———, ed. *The James Family.* New York: Vintage Books, 1980.

Menikoff, Barry. "Punctuation and Point of View in the Late Style of Henry James." *Style* 4 (1970):29–47.

Milic, Louis. "Theories of Style and Their Implications for the Teaching of Composition." In *Contemporary Essays on Style.* Ed. Glen A. Love and Michael Payne. Glenview, IL: Scott, Foresman, 1969.

Nisbett, Richard E., and Timothy Wilson. "Telling More Than We Know: Verbal Reports as Data." *Psychological Review* 84 (1977):231–59.

Nowell-Smith, Simon, ed. *The Legend of the Master.* New York: Scribner's, 1948.

Ohmann, Richard. "Generative Grammars and the Concept of Literary Style." In *Contemporary Essays on Style.* Ed. Glen A. Love and Michael Payne. Glenview, IL: Scott, Foresman, 1969.

———. "Mentalism in the Study of Literary Language." In *Proceedings of the Conference on Language and Language Behavior.* Ed. Eric M. Zale. New York: Appleton-Century- Crofts, 1968.

Page, Norman. *Henry James: Interviews and Recollections.* London: Macmillan, 1984.

Pascal, Roy. *The Dual Voice.* Manchester: Manchester Univ. Press, 1977.

Peinovich, Michael, and Richard Patteson. "The Cognitive Beast in the Syntactic Jungle: A Study of James' Language." *Language and Style* 11 (1978):82–93.

Ray, William. *Literary Meaning.* Oxford: Basil Blackwell, 1984.

Rosenblatt, Louise. *Literature as Exploration.* New York: Appleton-Century, 1938. Rev. ed.: Modern Language Association, 1983.

―――. *The Reader, The Text, The Poem.* Carbondale: Southern Illinois Univ. Press, 1978.

―――. "Transaction Versus Interaction—A Terminological Rescue Operation." *Research in the Teaching of English* 19 (1985):96–107.

Rumelhart, David. "Schemata: The Building Blocks of Cognition." In *Comprehension and Teaching: Research Reviews.* Ed. John T. Guthrie. Newark, NJ: International Reading Association, 1981.

Sebeok, Thomas, ed. *Style in Language.* Cambridge, MA: The MIT Press, 1960.

Short, R. W. "The Sentence Structure of Henry James." *American Literature* 18 (1946):71–88.

Shriber, Michael. "Cognitive Apparatus in *Daisy Miller, The Ambassadors,* and Two Works by Howells: A Comparative Study of the Epistemology of Henry James." *Language and Style* 2 (1969):207–25.

Sibley, Frank. "Aesthetic Concepts." In *Art and Philosophy.* Ed. W. E. Kennick. New York: St. Martin's, 1964.

Sloan, Gary. "Mistaking Subject Matter for Style." *College English* 43 (1981):502–7.

Slobin, Dan. *Psycholinguistics.* Glenview, IL: Scott, Foresman, 1971.

Smit, David W. "The Later Styles of Henry James." *Style* 21 (1987):95–106.

―――. "The Leap of the Beast: The Dramatic Style of Henry James' 'The Beast in the Jungle.'" *The Henry James Review* 4 (1983):219–30.

Smith, Barbara Herrnstein. *On the Margins of Discourse: The Relation of Literature to Language.* Chicago: The Univ. of Chicago Press, 1978.

Smith, William, F., Jr. "Sentence Structure in the Tales of Henry James." *Style* 7 (1973):157–72.

Spitzer, Leo. *Linguistics and Literary History: Essays in Stylisitics.* Princeton: Princeton Univ. Press, 1948.

Stanzel, Franz. *Narrative Situations in the Novel.* Trans. James P. Pusack. Bloomington: Indiana Univ. Press, 1971.

Steig, Michael. "Reading and Meaning." *College English* 44 (1982):182–89.

Stich, Steven P. *From Folk Psychology to Cognitive Science.* Cambridge, MA: The MIT Press, 1983.

Taylor, Gordon O. *The Passages of Thought: Psychological Representation in the American Novel 1870–1900.* New York: Oxford Univ. Press, 1969.

Taylor, Talbot J. *Linguistic Theory and Structural Stylistics.* New York: Pergamon Press, 1980.

Tomlinson, Barbara. "Talking About the Composing Process: The Limitations of Retrospective Accounts." *Written Communication* 1 (1984):429–45.

Tompkins, Jane P. "'The Beast in the Jungle': An Analysis of James' Late Style." *Modern Fiction Studies* 16 (1970): 185–91.

―――. "Criticism and Feeling." *College English* 39 (1977):169–78.

―――. "The Reader in History: The Changing Shape of Literary Response." In *Reader-Response Criticism.* Ed. Jane P. Tompkins. Baltimore: The Johns Hopkins Univ. Press, 1980.

Tormey, Alan. *The Concept of Expression: A Study in Philosophical Psychology and Aesthetics.* Princeton: Princeton Univ. Press, 1971.

Tracy, Bruce Philip. "Henry James' Representation of Inner Consciousness in

Meditation Scenes from the Late Novels." Diss. Michigan State University, 1971.

Veeder, William. *Henry James—The Lessons of the Master.* Chicago: The Univ. of Chicago Press, 1975.

Vivas, Eliseo. *Creation and Discovery.* Chicago: Henry Regnery, 1955.

Warren, Austin. *Rage for Order: Essays in Criticism.* Ann Arbor: The Univ. of Michigan Press, 1959.

Watanabe, Hisayoshi. "Past Perfect Retrospection in the Style of Henry James." *American Literature* 34 (1962):165–81.

Watt, Ian. "The First Paragraph of *The Ambassadors:* An Explication." In *Contemporary Essays on Style.* Ed. Glen A. Love and Michael Payne. Glenview, IL: Scott, Foresman, 1969.

Weathers, Winston. "The Rhetoric of the Series." In *Contemporary Essays on Style.* Ed. Glen A. Love and Michael Payne. Glenview: IL: Scott, Foresman, 1969.

Weaver, Richard. *The Ethics of Rhetoric.* Chicago: Henry Regnery, 1953.

Wellek, René. "Closing Statement." In *Style in Language.* Ed. Thomas Sebeok. Cambridge, MA: The MIT Press, 1960.

———. "Stylistics, Poetics, and Criticism." In *Literary Style: A Symposium.* Ed. Seymour Chatman. New York: Oxford Univ. Press, 1971.

———, and Austin Warren. *Theory of Literature.* 3d ed. New York: Harcourt, 1956.

Wilson, L. S. "The Stylistics of Henry James: A Linguistic Analysis of Selected Early and Late Novels." Diss. Florida State University, 1974.

Wilson, Timothy, Jay Hull, and Jim Johnson. "Awareness and Self- Perception: Verbal Reports on Internal States." *Journal of Personality and Social Psychology* 40 (1981):53–71.

Wimsatt, W. K. *The Verbal Icon.* Lexington: Univ. of Kentucky Press, 1954.

Wittgenstein, Ludwig. *Philosophical Investigations.* 2d ed. Trans. G.E.M. Anscombe. New York: Macmillan, 1968.

Index

David W. Smit, an assistant professor of English at Kansas State University, has published several articles on Jamesian style and stylistics. His principal research interests are reader response criticism, composition theory, and stylistics.